PROVENCE

A land of lavender and olives

The Traveler

Copyright © 2019 The Traveler
All rights reserved.

ISBN-13: 978-1-945858-12-3
ISBN-10: 1-945858-12-5

I wish to express my gratitude to our awesome host, Terry, and to my wonderful father and stepmother for giving me the opportunity to see France.

Great appreciation goes to God for making this marvelous and beautiful planet.

I thank all of you for your love.

France

Departure

Awaiting our ride, my father, stepmother, and I stood outside the front door of their home in Alexandria, Virginia. "Where is the taxi?" my stepmother, Carol, asked. "Call again. They must have canceled."

"Why would they cancel?" I looked at my phone as if it held the answer. "I just placed the request." Always finding it easier to comply with requests that don't hurt anybody, I called.

"Your taxi has been canceled. The driver could not find you and has been released. Press 1 to request a retry or 2 to cancel."

Curses, how hard could he have tried? We're standing outside with our luggage. I pressed 1. My phone immediately notified me that I had a new message. I clicked the texted link and watched our ride's progress toward our anxiously awaiting and completely visible bodies. "He's on Taney," I notified my family. "Oh no, he turned on Howard. That's not our street."

My father, who in my youth had removed a vicious shrew from the small, waterless, concrete pond in our backyard, now has difficulty standing or walking. He sat in the lawn chair by his front door and informed me, "He can get here that way too."

I stepped into the street. "The man should be able to see me out here. There he is!" I wind milled my arms like a wild woman. A black car with a white horizontal strip inched up the road. "Not very observant, is he?"

Finally seeing us, the driver hesitantly approached. *I guess I look too scary. He probably thinks I'm going to reach through his window and body slam him to the ground. Still, I don't blame him. Nowadays, one can't be too careful. Taxiing strangers has led to the brutal death of more than one taxi driver.*

Once on our way, I breathed a sigh of relief. I've never been to France, but I have a French ancestor who came to North America hundreds of ago, so I thought, *I wonder if the French DNA in me will know its home and be glad.*

At Reagan International airport, true to the agreement arranged through Dad's travel agent, a navigator stood ready with a wheelchair. Skillfully avoiding the mass of humanity, Carol and I scurried through the airport behind Dad. We rode the elevator then popped out a floor down. Adding to my happiness, we were escorted past the line snaking back and forth in front of the ticket counter. Cleared for travel, we were deposited at the gate. *I don't want to end up on a plane with terrorists planning to blow themselves, the plane, and all of us inside to smithereens. I hope they screen the rest of the people and their luggage carefully.*

Dad sat in his wheelchair. I, however, strolled to the gatekeeper and showed her my ticket. "We haven't even started boarding this plane that's going to Raleigh, NC."

I certainly don't want to get on that plane. "Thank you." I backed away and scanned the seating. *I guess we'll have to stand. I hope my back can take it.*

Blessedly, Carol had spent her time constructively finding empty chairs. "There are two seats over there."

"I'll roll Dad over."

"That's all right. I'll sit here. You go."

Half an hour later, we were first into the plane scheduled to fly us to the airport in New York. Dad slipped into his seat. "I hope they'll have the wheelchair ready when we get to JFK. That airport can be a mess."

I sat in my assigned aisle seat. *Wish I was next to the window. Maybe nobody is assigned to that one.*

A man interrupted my thoughts. "Excuse me. That's my seat over there."

Drat! I vacated my seat and allowed the man past me to my coveted location.

A moment later, a hostess leaned her head under the overhead storage compartment. "Sir, please feel free to move to your assigned seat in the row ahead."

Provence

My rival for the window seat replied, "No, thank you. I'm fine here."

I slightly twisted toward the man. "If you're not going to sit in your seat, maybe I will." I turned and spoke across the aisle. "Carol, I might move, I want to look out the window."

The man did not take the hint.

I unbuckled. One row forward, I sat beside a window and peered at the ocean and eastern shore of the United States. *It would be lovely if I saw a whale or dolphins, or even an ancient sea monster.*

No such luck, but we did land at JFK Airport on time. Unfortunately, to no benefit. The pilot's voice came over the speaker. "Our gate has not been vacated. We will have a thirty-minute wait." Forty minutes later, Dad called the hostess. "We have a connecting flight to catch. When will we be going to the gate?"

The woman flipped through the sheets of paper in her hands. With an accent so thick that her words were barely intelligible she asked, "What are your destination and flight number?" Dad supplied the information. "When you get off, turn right, and then get on bus to B18. Your gate is 22." She moved ahead and skillfully looked up information for the next couple. "You have only five minutes until your plane begins boarding." She quickly moved to the public address system. "Ladies and Gentlemen, if your final destination is New York, please remain seated and allow the people with connections to make quick egress."

Finally at the gate, the fasten seatbelts sign went off. Those of us believing we would immediately exit, hurriedly pulled our carry-ons from the overhead compartments. We then stood in the aisle for five minutes, waiting for the door to open. The couple going to Germany dashed off the plane and scurried away. *I hope they make their flight.*

Just outside the plane door, in the exit tunnel, stood a young Frenchman with a wheelchair. He said something in French.

I had no idea what the man had said. I knew Dad didn't either. I interjected, "He speaks English."

"Please state your name," the man repeated his previous words, this time in English.

Dad did so.

"I am here for you. Please get in."

In the exit tunnel, the young man paused long enough to kiss the cheek of a young hostess headed into the plane we had vacated. *They must be lovers.* My thoughts shifted. *I'm sure this man already know where he's supposed to take us.* I stated the information anyway. "We need to take the bus to B18 and then get to gate 22." Weaving through the crowd, I speed-walked to keep pace. Somehow still last to get on the full bus, I thought, *how did everybody else already get here?* It then occurred to me, *we must have made an earlier bus than the one meant for our plane. All the better.* In his wheelchair, Dad rolled in. His footrests pressed against the legs of the people already in seats. My stepmother and I crammed in behind and clung to the hold bar. Two quick stops and we were at B18. The driver dilly-dallied with his phone. "Deploy the ramp," I ordered him, "We have to get the wheelchair out."

He complied.

On a less crowded and less traveled corridor, I avoided the glances of the envious as we raced to gate 22. Once safely seated on the large intercontinental airplane headed to Nice, France, I thought with eager anticipation, *I'll soon be on my way to a part of the planet I've never seen.*

I was wrong. We sat on the tarmac, not getting even one millimeter closer to our destination. Thirty long minutes later, the voice of the Captain came over the intercom. "We have been notified that our flight has again been delayed. We anticipate another thirty-minute delay."

Hurry and wait. The Great American Way! Sixty long minutes passed. Night fell. *Surely, we'll leave soon.*

"We have been cleared for takeoff."

France

Happy days!

Then the following words filled my ears, "We are fifteenth in line. We estimate takeoff in thirty minutes."

We crept down the taxi lane. We paused. We shifted another notch forward. *Goodness, how time does not pass when you're waiting.*

Finally, a smooth takeoff, only an hour and fifteen minutes behind schedule. The Captain announced, "We have a tailwind of 89 knots per hour. We should arrive in Nice on schedule."

We'll see.

In a center seat, and not able to see anything but darkness on the other side of the window, I decided to watch a movie on the tiny screen before me.

The hostess interrupted my search. "Pasta, chicken, or chicken salad?"

"What kind of pasta?"

"It's ravioli."

I accepted my tray with prepackaged-heated-in-a-microwave ravioli, a small garden salad, a cold roll, butter, a container with three grapes, two slices of cheese, and two Captain's Wafers. Beside them sat a plastic-wrapped fudge brownie. I popped a grape into my mouth and settled in to watch "Adrift."

The movie ended. I turned off the monitor, grabbed my blanket and a few small airplane pillows, and tried to find three empty seats together. All occupied. *Drat.* I moved back to the two-seat space across from Dad and attempted to fit in the small space. That proved to be impossible.

Provence

Arrival

After a sleepless night, the hostess arrived with breakfast. I looked at my tray: yogurt, a cold muffin, and a piece of packaged cheese. Nothing but the yogurt tasted good. With a spoonful in my mouth, I selected another movie. "Solo." *I've been wanting to watch that.* Before the movie had ended, we were flying low over the French Riviera. I paused the movie. As I filmed the beach, the movie service ended. Sadly, I don't know if Han and Kara got to stay together or even survived their dire predicament.

Again escorted past long customs lines, our passports were looked over and then stamped. We hoped to quickly find the woman Carol had befriended then roomed with more than fifty years before when they had worked together at the World Bank. The door opened, "There she is! There's Terry!" My stepmother exclaimed. Our wonderful wheelchair operator stood by as hugs and cheek kisses were exchanged. He then pushed my father all the way to our friend's car.

With the three of us safely ensconced in her Peugeot, Terry skillfully backed out of the hemmed in parking space. A two-point maneuver later, the car pointed forward with a clear path ahead. Off we went. Twice, we circled a stone giant as we attempted to identify the correct exit ramp. Having successfully escaped the busy airport, I endured the nerve-wracking stop and go, and swerving of navigating Nice traffic. I focused on the mountains. "Is all of France so full of mountains?"

"Yes, I'll take you to see some spectacular mountains tomorrow." Terry jerked the steering wheel and skillfully avoided a collision. We safely made it out of the city then traveled a curving road past Draguignan. Then up, up, and up into the mountains. At our mountaintop destination, Saint-Pierre de Tourtour, Terry drove under the community's stone arch entryway. "Look to your left. You see how the earth looks under those pines? Wild boar tore up the ground digging for things to eat."

"Wow! I hope I'll get to see some."

Terry's beautiful house nestled into the mountainside with a gorgeous view of the valley and mountain ranges in the far distance.

France

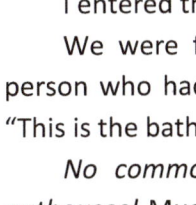

I entered the pale yellow house with a terra cotta roof.

We were first introduced to the room, most vital to a person who had just taken a long ride. Terry opened a door. "This is the bathroom."

No commode! That's not good. Surely they don't use outhouses! Much to my relief, the second door opened into a narrow room with the necessary equipment and a tiny sink.

The house was full of marvelous angles, curves, and patterns of light and shadow.

Provence

The beautiful furniture looked inviting.

France

We sat on the patio that overlooked the valley. Dad's eyes brimmed with tears. "It's so peaceful here. Do you see why I wanted to come? I thought I was never going to see this again."

Before long, we were talking, laughing, and eating thin slices of ham, chunks of blue cheese, and slices of French bread washed down with a lovely rosé wine.

Provence

That night, strips of yellow, orange, and pink faded into the purple mountains. *How could anybody believe this beauty came into existence through random mutations?*

France

Gorges du Verdon

I sat on the back porch sipping hot Fennel tea as the sun rose. *What's that?!* I heard a rustling in the backyard hedge. A red nose peeked out from under the bush and sniffed the air. *It's the fox Terry told us about last night. I'll be able to see it better when it passes that open area farther up.* I watched the hedge intently. The rustling drew nearer. Again, the long snout appeared. Suddenly, the fox dashed across the neighbor's yard. To my dismay, on the wrong side of the hedge. *Oh well, at least I saw its nose and a flash of red fur.*

On the other side of an open wall, my stepmother stepped from her bedroom through the French doors onto the porch.

"I saw the fox," I informed her.

"Maybe I'll get to see it too."

"Probably not. It ran around the neighbor's pool then kept right on going."

Answering my stepmother's wish, the fox soon returned. Just as she had quickly spotted Terry in the airport, she saw the animal step out of the hedge into our hostess's yard. "There it is!"

In full view, it stopped and posed with one foot up. Unafraid, it looked at us then continued its leisurely stroll across Terry's backyard. Both of us happy with our reward for getting up early, we finished our cereal and toast as Dad and Terry joined us.

Off we went in Terry's hybrid car. My thoughtful stepmother offered, "Fill up your tank. I'll pay for the gas." Unable to make her credit card work for the 69 € charge, Dad passed his wife his card. I dug out my phone and started the calculator. *$78.72! European gas prices are insane*. Having a good reason to conserve gasoline, we did not turn on the air conditioning. Instead, we rode with the windows slightly down.

Terry rounded another sharp curve in the twisting road. "This is what we call the Grand Canyon of the Verdon River."

We drew closer and closer to the gray mountains riddled with yellowish-pink veins that loomed ahead. Up and up into the massive mountain, we twisted along the narrow road. Not wanting to go over the edge, each time a car came from the opposite direction, we stopped and let it pass. I knew squeezing the door armrest would be of no help if our car did leave the road, I clutched it tightly anyway.

"This is the first overlook." Terry pulled into a small overview.

Provence

I carted my camera to the precipice. My head swooned as I peered at the Verdon River far below. From the dizzying heights, I couldn't judge the distance. *Certainly, I'd reach terminal velocity long before I splattered against the rocks below.* I clutched the handrail even tighter than I had the armrest in the car.

"There are ropes over here." My stepmother pointed to the opposite side of the railing.

I looked at the ropes tied to rings driven into the rock. "They must be for repelling, that's something I wouldn't want to do, at least not here."

Click. Click. I captured the image of the bright teal water far below before we loaded up and continued along the edge of the giant gorge through the limestone.

We came to a tunnel cut into a mountain prominence. "You want to stop to take a picture?" Terry asked.

It's very unlikely that I'll ever be here again, but then again, it wasn't likely that I'd be here now. Still, I should do what I can with what I have right now. I may not be able to do so later. Guess I'll teeter at the edge of the gorge again. "Yes, please."

Dad and I looked into the hole through the solid rock. He leaned against the stones. Then, with more pictures in my smartphone, I climbed back into the car. We entered the short tunnel followed by a longer one with windows cut to the outside to allow in the light.

France

Stop after stop, I daringly stood at the edges of the precipices and snapped pictures. Carol advised me, "You still have a long time before we leave, you should ration your pictures."

"I'll download the photos to my computer. I'll have plenty of space to take more."

Later that day, we arrived in the village Aiguines.

We walked up the sidewalk to Restaurant Terrasse. Terry asked, "Would you like to eat inside?"

"Outside," Dad replied.

We rounded an ancient fountain. Terry and Carol went to the chalkboard by the door to discover the daily special.

Provence

My father and I took a seat in the shade of one of the large Sycamore tree.

Soon, a handsome, young man from South Africa came to our table. "I will be your waiter."

Dad decided on the special. Because I want to stay in the boundaries of expense that my parents find appropriate, I ordered the same.

The waiter asked me, "How do you want your meat?"

Not knowing the proper French words, I decide on a more descriptive approach. "Not cold and red. Not hot and brown. I want warm pink."

In French, Terry spoke a word. I assumed how she thought I wanted the meat prepared. The waiter replied, "No Madame. Not the way she described it."

Terry insisted, "I know what she wants."

"Very well."

Once prepared, the waiter brought my steak. "Please try and let me know if your meat is prepared correctly."

I cut a small chunk and popped the perfectly warm, pink beef into my mouth. "Exactly!"

Proud of himself for getting my request right, in French, the waiter named the way I like a beefsteak: 'moyen bien'.

Dad tasted the meat on his plate. I noticed tears welling up in his eyes. *Maybe father feels his life is ending. He's so nostalgic and emotional about things. I think he wants to repeat the things he's enjoyed in his past. I'm glad I was able to come, so he could too.*

I took another bite of steak smothered in white wine sauce. "I'd like to go to the castle."

"We can go over and see if it's open. Most likely the season has ended." Terry asked the waiter, "When does this restaurant close for the winter?"

"At the end of the week?"

It's Thursday. Probably the castle is closed.

As I finished the last of my scalloped potatoes, our waiter approached our table. "Would you care for dessert?" he asked.

I don't know why. I couldn't have read it. I glanced around to see if there was a menu. "What do you have?"

"Crème Caramel or a Strawberry tarte."

"Dad," I asked, "would you like to order one and I the other then both of us have half of each?"

"Good idea." Dad ordered, "Crème Caramel."

I, therefore, requested, "Strawberry tarte."

Shortly after ordering, the waiter brought a wedge of crispy crust covered with chunks of fresh strawberries that glittered in the sunlight reflecting off the sugar coating. Having been raised to get the last piece if I was the person dividing the food, I carefully cut the wedge exactly in half. Once I had enjoyed my portion of the delicious berries, Dad and I exchanged plates. I savored the smooth caramel covered custard.

France

As we neared the castle gate, it became clear that the building was indeed closed. Instead of going into the castle, I visited its tiny plot of land allocated to the dead. As I stood in the cemetery, I admired the colored tiles of the castle turrets surrounded by a cloudless blue sky then changed my focus and looked at the vineyards below.

We drove the ups, downs, and twists of the road as we descended through olive groves to the Verdon River's exit from the gorges into Lac de Saint Croix. On foot, I made my way to the center of the bridge. My camera flashed fifteen percent battery life remaining. I snapped a photo of a microscopic swimmer on the beach below then hurried across the road and took a picture of the bright teal water gently flowing from the gap.

At the sound of a loud buzzing, every person on the bridge turned his head. Out of the gorge came a drone. I waved. As if to acknowledge my greeting, it flew close then stopped not far from me. Filming away, my battery gave out. *I should have listened to my stepmother.* I stuffed my dead smartphone into my hip pouch and returned to the car.

Provence

Next stop: the 12th-century village of Moustiers-Sainte-Marie. Pipes spewed spring water at the many fountains. Grape vines so old and large that I barely got my hands around them with the very tips of my fingers touching, trailed their branches down the narrow streets. Their leaves provided shade over the benches where tourists rested from their struggle to make it up and down the sloping cobblestone paths.

An enticing scent drew me into a small shop. Clutching sachets of flowers made from the extensive nearby lavender fields, I examined the world-renowned faience pottery. I remained true to my fascination with elephants. A small one painted with the traditional heron design caught my attention and then joined my collection.

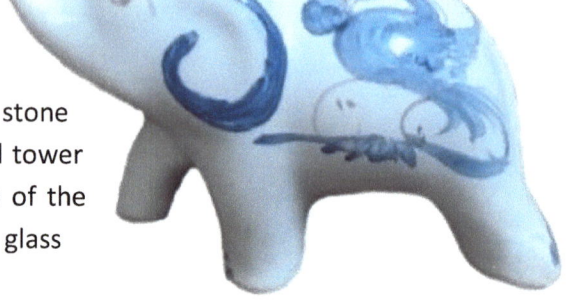

I carted my treasures beyond massive oak doors then down stone stairs into the dim coolness of the 13th century church whose bell tower decayed above me. I strolled past the nave containing a statue of the Virgin Mary and Child. I gazed at the church's large stained glass window.

This wasn't an ordinary village. That's quite a symbol of the wealth this village had when this church was built. I wish my phone hadn't died. I traced my steps back to the place I had entered. I spoke to Terry. "I want to go out the lower door."

"All right," Terry told me, "We will meet you on the other street." She ascended the upper stairs.

I dipped my finger in the Holy Water at the lower entrance. *I'm not Catholic, but a blessing is a blessing.* I rubbed a wet cross on my forehead.

With Holy Water glistening above my eyebrows, I picked up a tester bottle of perfume in the store beside the church. *French perfume and Holy Water all at the same time. I wonder what that will do.* I sprayed perfume onto my wrists and sniffed. *Smells nice and not too strong! I hope I don't blow up or melt down or something.*

Outside the perfume shop, I informed the others, "I just applied a quick spray of perfume on my wrists, and I have Holy Water on my forehead."

Dad joked, "Then they should definitely let you into Heaven."

I'm glad Dad saw it that way. I love him.

We made the long uphill hike back to the parking lot. I gazed at the other church hundreds of stairs up but still far below the star hanging from a chain strung from one mountain peak to the opposite peak. *I'd like to go to the church way up there, but the climb would probably kill me. How on earth did they string that chain across there?* Knowing I wasn't going to find out even if I could survive the ascent, I climbed into Terry's car.

Back and forth on hairpin turns, we passed masses of olive trees. We drove past never-ending rows of lavender plants shaved down to green buttons as the purple flowers had been harvested — the fields so big that the rows curved over the low rolling hills and then disappeared. Beyond, the groves of olives that again grew beside the road, we stopped at the final wayside to look back across the lake at the villages on the opposite hillside. As I walked back to the car, I read the sign in front of the orchard before me. "Truffles?"

Terry passed on her knowledge. "The fungus grows on the roots of these trees. Remember how the wild boar dug up the ground under the pines by my house?"

"I do."

"Pigs can smell what's under the ground. They train them to find the truffles."

"I didn't know pigs were that smart." – Wild boars are called 'sangliers' in French. –

France

We rode away through more fields of Lavender. "Oh look!" I exclaimed. "That field surrounded by sunflowers reminds me of that Van Gogh print in Terry's house."

At our final stop, the wine store in Aups, Terry, my stepmother, and I sampled a rosé and then a red wine. Terry bought a box of each. I bought a bottle of Rosé to share with my husband, once home. We stepped out of the shop.

"Look at those clouds. Aren't they strange?" I sniffed the air. "It smells like smoke."

"Those definitely aren't normal looking clouds and look at the white clouds above the gray ones rolling over the top of the mountains." Terry stuck her key into the ignition slot.

We discussed the odd clouds on the way home. "Maybe you can ask somebody if there's a fire somewhere?" Dad suggested.

In the house, Terry turned on the television to see if there was any information in the news. "Why isn't this working?" After an hour of fiddling, she gave up. "I guess we won't find out today."

Provence

A Day of Rest

Carol asked, "Lisa, do you want to walk to the restaurant and see if they serve lamb?"

"Sure," I agreed. Off we went. At the foot of the hill, wild boar had again dug up the ground around the pine trees. *I hope I'll get to see some of those pigs, but not too close, I don't want to be gored.* We strolled under the stone arch then across the street.

"Georges," my stepmother called out.

From around the side of the building, we heard a reply, so we headed that way. I stood alongside Carol. The man spoke in French, looked at me from time to time, and laughed. *I'm sure he's saying something funny. I should be laughing.* Since I had not a clue as to what was being said, I only smiled. *Most likely, I appear to be an idiot.*

Carol updated me as we walked away. "He never has lamb chops, but he does have leg of lamb all the time."

"That sounds good to me."

Back at Terry's, Carol passed on the information. We all agreed that leg of lamb was more than acceptable. Terry phoned in a noon reservation for four people the coming Sunday.

That means we won't be doing any sightseeing on Sunday. Drat.

"Lisa, will you help me get this television working?" Terry requested.

Since IT support is what I do for a living, I set to troubleshooting. I checked the cable connections and the power strips. "Everything is plugged in and on. Did you say this decoder box has a card in it?"

Terry popped out the card. "It's expired. I'll call them Monday and get another. We could watch a DVD about Provence."

"All right."

Terry found the correct disk and slid it into the slot. 'Loading' displayed on the screen.

After a long wait, Terry said, "Maybe I need to go ahead and press play." She pressed a button. Nothing changed. She then attempted to stop the disk and pressed the stop button. Nothing changed. Next, she tried to eject it. The player continued to display 'loading.' She flipped the surge strip off then on. As soon as the machine turned back on, she pressed the eject button.

"Wonderful, you got your disk out!"

She stuck it back into the machine!

Why did she do that? I asked myself.

The DVD player had not changed its electronic mind about the disk. Again, it informed us that it was loading. *Unfortunately, that machine is not able to change tenses. Too bad. I would have liked to have seen, loaded.*

Terry went through the off/on/press eject procedure several times before she forced the DVD player to again release the disk. "I want to try one more time," she informed me.

"Try a different disk," I suggested.

We got the same results with the second disk. When Terry tried the third, she got one second of a picture.

"I think your DVD player has gone bad." *So much for watching television.*

In the afternoon, we again walked the road beside Terry's house. This time, we went the other direction.

France

Not far up the hill, at the end of the street, we came to a couple of small ponds.

Frogs leaped into the water as I approached. I saw no fish. I did, however, see plenty of cattails.

Provence

I examined a mud pit at the edge of the pond. "I bet this was mucked up by those wild pigs."

"I agree." My father lowered himself to a low cement bench. "You all go on. I can see the ponds from here." Tears again welled up into his eyes. "I collected dragonflies and damselflies at the pond's dam."

My father is a world-renowned entomologist specializing in Trichoptera, an insect that looks like a small brown moth. I asked, "What about Caddisflies?"

"None."

My stepmother, Terry, and I circumnavigated the body of water before returning to the bench.

"Dad, pull up holding my hands." I held mine out.

"Let me get my feet situated." Dad drew his feet in close. Terry and I braced as he raised himself up. We held on until he was steady.

Walking back to Terry's, we stopped every few minutes for Dad to get his breath. Time and congestive heart failure have changed the man whose long strides down the sidewalks of Washington D.C. had required my childhood legs to run to keep pace.

At dinner, which consisted of bread, cheese, apples, and soup made of leeks, thyme, and ground greens, Terry informed us, "There are some Roman ruins we could see."

"That sounds lovely. I'd love to see them." *I hope I'll get to see more of France than the inside of Terry's home.* Outside, not even the valley below was visible through the rain.

France

Aups

Flashes of lightning and rolls of thunder filled the night. The morning sounds of people moving about woke me. Today, we're going to the farmer's market in Aups. A real French village not altered to attract tourists. After that, perhaps the Museum of Ancient History or the Roman ruins. I got out from under the warm comforter and looked at my phone. *8:15 already! We're supposed to leave at 9.* Dad, Carol, and I vied for the bathroom. Being me, I compliantly waited then took the fastest shower I could and threw on my clothes. I gulped a breakfast of yogurt, a banana, fennel tea, and a slice of toast with Rhubarb jam.

Off we went. Me, with the still blank postcards I had purchased in Moustiers Sainte-Marie. I attempted to write as we swerved and bounced, or screeched to a halt at every passing car. One postcard is for my sons. The other for my husband; with a French postmark; the evidence that I truely am in France.

I discovered that we are to have Monique and Robar over for a late birthday party for Dad and Carol. The time of the celebration set for lunch. Therefore, we are not going to the museum or the Roman ruins. I followed Terry's quick steps to the post office, then sat at a small table and completed my postcard. Since I have not been able to exchange any of my American money, I pulled out my card.

Terry spoke up. "It's a very small amount and not worth using your card. I'll get them." She graciously bought me two stamps.

I licked and stuck them to the cards. "Merci." I handed them to the postal clerk.

Terry informed me, "They won't be postmarked from here. They'll be marked at the central office."

"That's all right. The postmark will be French."

Next up was the bakery. A young fellow, about six years old, walked toward me. In a paper bag, he proudly carried a long, slender loaf of bread spanning an inch above his toes to a few inches above the top of his head. *How adorable!* I pulled out my phone to snap a photo. T*hat's a bad idea. His father probably wouldn't like me taking a picture of his son.* I let them pass, only to be remembered in my mind.

Terry stepped into the small bakery. She bought two loaves of bread, and a pastry whose ingredients were described to her.

I, however, remained ignorant as I contemplated the value of sampling two actual French Éclairs versus the unwanted calories and disapproval of others.

Two men stepped up to the counter and placed their orders. *Oh well, I shouldn't eat them anyway.* Both men completed their purchases. Terry still remained in the store fiddling with her purse. *I'll get one for everybody and not feel so guilty.* I slid to the counter and held up four fingers. "Éclairs."

Provence

"Which kind?" the sales clerk asked in English.

Guess my ignorance is pretty obvious. Two eclairs in the display case had a layer of chocolate and two a layer of caramel down the center of the top. Assuming the filling in all of them was custard I said, "Chocolate."

"I have only two chocolate."

"All right then, just the two."

The intelligent young lady packaged them in a box, which she tied up with a ribbon. I handed her my card, signed the paper, and then carried my guilty treat out of the store along with Terry's circular pastry, also tied up in a box.

On to the yarn store where Terry bought a piece of elastic band. I admired the soft, beautiful yarn but followed her out without a purchase of my own. "Let's find your father," Terry led me past a table with salad forks and spoons made from local olive trees. Beside them, a sack of walnuts lay on its side, spilling its contents.

Large Chestnuts as well as packages of fennel and thyme were piled up for our viewing, and I'm sure, purchasing pleasure. We hurried past baskets for sale and Clementines. I eyeballed the seafood on ice, including the squishy, off-white mass of squid.

We also didn't stop at the food stand on my left that offered delicious smelling paella with large shrimp heads, sticking out of orange couscous. Nor did I stop for the stamped-out sheets of small ravioli squares or the bright red stuffed tomatoes. We also passed a flower stand displaying a wild mix of colors and then the mattress and pillow stand.

France

Terry pointed across the busy street. "There he is." She left me with my father as she went for the car.

Dad and I returned to the market to find my stepmother. I'm sure Dad didn't know I had previously admired the olive wood salad utensils, which I had not attempted to buy. Terry had told me they only take cash. An unhappy disadvantage of Aups not being a tourist town. In Moustiers-Sainte-Marie, all the shops had been prepared to take a credit card. Dad held up a set. "These would make a good souvenir."

"They only take cash. I'll trade you American dollars for some of your Euros."

"We'll figure out the money later." Dad bought me a set.

We found Carol and turned back. She stopped at a vendor stand. "Look at these umbrellas. There are pictures on them." The vendor demonstrated how one closed inside out, leaving the image still visible while not in use. Carol remarked, "How nice," but continued on without one.

We three waited at the side of the road, the only place our ride could stop. While we stood at the edge of the market, a man attempted to sell Carol tree care services. She took the flyer. Glad to have a reason, she stepped away to Terry's Peugeot, which blocked the road. I ignored the honking as I opened the rear hatch and deposited our purchases. Dad struggled to get his feet through the door too small for quick access.

I hope nobody comes over here and clobbers me. Finally, totally inside, I closed Dad's door and quickly jumped in. We sped off to the wine store.

Dad had enjoyed the rosé so much that he wanted to buy another box. Not under pressure to exit quickly, he slowly got out of the car and then made his way into the store. Glad that he was able to do so, he carried the box of wine to the car.

On the road to Terry's home, I noticed groves with two-foot-high stumps of old olive trees, each with a large sucker or two covered with ripening fruit.

A wide bus barreled down on us. Due to the problem of driving on a very narrow road, Terry once again applied the brakes. As far to the edge as possible, we waited for the monstrosity to zip past. The driver flashed the headlights to thank us for the space. Safely back at Terry's house, I headed to my room to deposit my treasures.

Terry prepared a lovely lunch of sweet radishes made into roses that she served with butter and salt. The second course consisted of yummy fried scallops, fried leeks, fried mushrooms, bread, and cheese. For dessert, Terry served the lemon chess pie she had purchased at the bakery in Aups.

The rest of the day, we tried to help Carol access her email. I finally convinced her that she was not going to be able to do so because she had not brought her cell phone to receive the required access code. We again tried to determine why the TV, satellite, nor DVD worked. After much troubleshooting, Terry decided that her DVD player did indeed need to be replaced and gave up. We all got out our books and read.

After a dinner of green beans and, you guessed it – bread, cheese, and wine, I excused myself to my room to read a message from my husband.

Provence

Les Pins Tranquilles

Today is Sunday. The day of our lunch reservation at Les Pins Tranquilles.

Carol knocked on my door. "Lisa, come help me. There's no water coming out of the faucet."

I fiddled with the knobs. They turned, but not a single drop of water flowed. We got Terry. She fiddled. She sprayed vinegar on the knobs. The spout still spewed no water. "I'll see if the gardener will look at this when he comes tomorrow."

I'm glad I showered yesterday. I left Carol to take a sponge bath with water from the sink.

Fog filled the valley. Drizzle and coldness filled the mountain air. I passed the morning inside, reading.

At noon, we made our way to the restaurant. The sign on the door flipped from closed to open as we approached. Inside, abstracts of women, splashes of colors suggesting bosoms and legs akimbo, hung on the walls. All paintings by the father of Georges, the restaurant owner.

We sat at a table beside a large window. Outside, tables on an uncovered patio were wet with rain. In the corner of the room, an open fireplace crackled. Georges arrived at our table with a large silver tray. The edges of a sheet of white paper showed around its edges. He tilted the tray. On the paper, lay four large slices of mutton.

"Très bien." Terry accepted the meat.

To my surprise, Georges, who is also the chef, carried the tray to the fireplace. I heard the meat sizzle. "Is he cooking it over there?" I asked.

"Yes, Georges is famous for cooking meat perfectly on his fire."

I don't think that's going to happen. It's not easy to regulate the flames of an open fire. The others looked over the menu. I told my father, "You'll have to select something for me. I have no idea what any of this is."

Dad stated the choices. "Salad of tomatoes or salad of anchovies."

"Tomatoes," I requested.

Terry waved for our waitress. "A bottle of the house wine."

Before she opened the wine, the attractive lady placed a purple bottle of water on the table.

I picked up the water. "Which glass?" No reply. *I'm probably doing this wrong, but oh well.* I poured water into the large glass before me.

Our server returned to our table. "No, Madame, that glass is for the wine."

That figures! I drank some then transferred the remainder into the small glass.

"The wine must breathe." She tipped the bottle. The dark, red liquid flowed into the proper receptacle.

I sipped the wine as if I knew how to be a connoisseur and waited for somebody else to pick up the proper implement to take an olive or pepperoni slice from the small platter on the other side of the wine and water bottles. After Carol had retrieved an olive with a toothpick, I stabbed then savored a black olive soaked in its oil with spices then also sampled a thin slice of red meat. "Tastes like pepperoni only smoother."

"And not as hard," Dad added.

A festival of red tomatoes surrounding a leafy core of greens was placed before me. "Looks delightful."

The waitress brought only one fork and one knife. *I don't even have to figure out which eating utensil.*

France

I swallowed my last bite of flavor-filled tomato. With impeccable timing, my grilled-to-perfection mutton with a slice of crispy French bread, roasted endive, a tiny salad, and sautéed mushrooms, arrived.

The tender mutton melted in my mouth. *Georges indeed deserves his fame. He has perfectly cooked this meat over his open fire.* French fries of potatoes that tasted heavenly and bread with a soft middle and crunchy crust accompanied the meal. As if all that were not enough, we also enjoyed dessert: pear sorbet, passion fruit sorbet, and flaming Crème Brûlée.

Returning to the table, Terry passed on the news she had just been told. "There was an explosion at the military facility. They let it burn out on its own. That was the smoke we saw when we were coming home from the Gorges du Verdon."

Provence

The Dinner Party

The rain poured on the other side of the wooden shutters I had fastened shut to stop them from banging in the wind. *I wonder if I'll see cracks of light when the sun comes up. If it's already day, I might not even know it with all this rain. I doubt the gardener will be coming. No faucet repairs. Oh, well.* I dropped back into sleep.

Sometime later, I again opened my eyes. Slits of light shone in around the edges of the heavy shutters. *This time it is morning. If I get up now, I might see the fox again.* I dressed then slipped out the kitchen door to the porch. I patiently waited as the coolness of the morning settled into my slippered feet.

From inside the warm house, Terry said, "Good morning, Lisa."

That fox is smart enough to stay in its den and out of this rain. I guess I'll go inside. "Good morning." I put my feet back onto the cold ceramic tiles of the patio.

Terry opened the door. "I've made you fennel tea."

I gratefully accepted the teapot filled with warmth. I carried it, along with a bowl of brown sugar rounds, to the dining table.

"Today's a day for reading books." Terry followed with a tray of bread and lavender honey.

Soon, Terry, Carol, Dad, and I sat at the table. I smeared pork pâté on a slice of hard French bread. "What time are your guests coming, Terry?"

"One o'clock."

I made my way to the couch. The day progressed as I read. That afternoon, the mouth-watering aroma of cooking Guinea Hen floated from the kitchen.

"Oliver," Terry asked, "would you carve?"

Slipping on an apron, my Dad complied.

The doorbell rang. "Bonjour," Terry's first guest stepped out of the rain. Only a few minutes later, the other guests joined us. Out of their wet coats, they sat in the living room surrounded by orchids.

"Which one would you like?" Terry held a bottle of Crème de Cassis and another of Pineau des Charentes. I selected Cassis: a blackcurrant liquor. I sampled a small sip. *This is so thick. It's unpleasant. Watering down is definitely necessary.* I added water from the carafe placed on the table for that very purpose. We ate carrots, cherry tomatoes, cauliflower, and dip. The conversation was lively, unfortunately, all in French. I had not one clue what was said, but laughter filled the room, and I enjoyed being a part of the festivities.

France

Only one tomato remained when Terry seated us at her table in front of the large French doors. My father sat at the table's end with me to his left. Since neither of us speaks French, that was a good plan. We could have spoken to each other, instead, we pretended to hang on every word spoken by Terry's guests.

Our plates, brought hot from the oven to keep the food warm, were positioned on those already on the table in front of us. I assumed so that we did not burn our hands. Terry's friend, Gisele, portioned the guinea hen onto each plate and then added a spoonful of potatoes. Flavors of thyme and sage tantalized my tongue, followed by creamy slices of potatoes cooked with onions and garlic. Red and rosé wines flowed.

Teary-eyed, my father complimented the French people who had treated him respectfully when his slow descent had blocked foot traffic at one of the Verdon Grand Canyon overlooks. Terry graciously translated the message.

Once the delectable fare had been consumed, Terry cleared the table of plates and glasses. Dad, however, tenaciously held on to his glass of Rosé. Terry placed champagne flutes, small plates, and small forks before each of us then brought out the treat brought by a guest. Gisele divided out her desert of thinly, sliced apples and strawberries baked in brown sugar.

As dessert was served, Alan loosened the wire of a champagne bottle. He attempted to prevent the cork from becoming a flying object and kept his hand over it.

POP!

Unhindered by Alan, the cork flew away. Happily, it missed his wife, Monique. Alan filled the flutes. In anticipation of what was to come, Dad released his empty wine glass.

"I can't get everybody into the photo." Terry climbed onto a stool to get the needed angle.

Before the last bite was gone, Terry asked, "Who wants coffee? Lisa, would you like herbal tea?"

Like magic, coffee cups were placed, then filled. Halfway to the bottom of my teacup, Terry brought out rum from Saint Martinique and seven shot glasses.

The people who had to drive home declined.

25

Provence

I, however, was already in the house where I would spend the night. I poured a tablespoonful into my tiny glass and sampled.

Terry's guests prepared to go home. I suggested, "Terry, maybe Alan would look at the tub faucets." A few minutes later, all the guests had left. "Was he able to fix them?" I asked.

"He didn't need to. He turned the knobs, and the water came out."

I tried them several times and never got a drop. I marched to the bathroom and turned the knob. Water flowed into the tub. *That's so strange!*

Thank you, Terry, for the elegant meal, and thank you, Alan, for your magic faucet knob rotating ability.

France

Saint-Michel Du Var and Tourtour Catholic Church

Standing in my bedroom in the morning light, I peered out the open window. *What?!* Snow sat on the rooftops, the grass, and the bushes. The rising sun warmed the air. Melting snow dripped everywhere.

Carol and Terry had planned to leave early to join a hiking group. Expecting to find only my father still in the house, I opened my door. Carol stood in the hall, looking at an old map replica hanging on the wall. "You're still here. Is it early?" I asked.

"We didn't go. The snow must have canceled it."

I left my stepmother in the hall, turned the tub faucet knobs, and received water. I love a bath. I refuse to give up the relaxation. I filled the narrow tub, crammed my arms against my sides, and squeezed in. Once squeaky clean, I dressed then joined the others at the table.

Terry informed us. "We'll walk by the pond then take a long walk in the woods."

Ducks swam in the almost overflowing pond. Beside the water, happy from the previous day's heavy rain, their babies waddled over. *They must think we'll give them bread.* Since we had nothing to give them, we left them behind.

Provence

On the far side of the pond, we met a couple with small children. The oldest child asked, "Do you want to see mushrooms?" She led us in loops until she relocated the bright yellow caps she had stomped to smithereens.

After circling the pond, we rejoined my father at the bench. "This is the only place I ever found any Caddisflies," he informed us.

We made our way back to Terry's Peugeot, slowly exited the parking lot over bumpy stones, and then drove to the other side of the St. Pierre complex on a freshly tarred and graveled road.

My dad did not exit the car when we again parked. "You all go on. I'll putter around by the car."

Happy to take a long walk, Carol started up the rocky trail. Terry and I followed, leaving my dad in a field of yellow and rust colored bracken.

A short way along, Terry broke a few leaves off a plant beside the road. "Do you know what this is?" She crushed the leaves and held them under my nose.

"Rosemary!" I looked at the plants along the road. "It grows wild out here?"

Yes," she replied.

I crushed and sniffed leaves as I walked.

Seemingly out of nowhere, a dog joined us. *I hope that boxer isn't vicious. There isn't anywhere to go. Best to act friendly.* I held my hand slightly out with the back forward. It sniffed me, and then gently licked my hand. It examined Carol and then Terry. Accompanied by the dog, we continued on. "It must live around here and heard us."

France

A voice called out. The dog dashed to the people rounding the bend behind us. Without saying a word, the horse riders turned onto a side trail. With only its flag of a tail visible, the dog that was much more friendly than the people, followed them away.

Further ahead, I spotted a tree blind. "People must use that to hunt wild boar."

Terry pointed above the wooden structure. "How do you call it? You kiss under it at the New Year."

"Mistletoe!" I surveyed the forest. "It's everywhere."

We trekked on. The trail dead-ended at a tee in the path. In the woods in front of us, sat a large metal tank pained blue.

"Why haul trash out here?"

Terry explained, "These are fire roads. That's a tank of water. There's no other place to get any way out here. The firemen know the locations of all the tanks."

"Oh, that makes sense." I followed along the fire road up a gentle slope. The trees on the left opened to reveal the landscape beyond.

"Over there is the military facility where they had the explosion."

I looked at what appeared as virgin land. "I see nothing except forest."

Provence

After snapping a photo, we went on. "Not much further you'll see an incredible view."

I hope we're getting close. I obediently continued walking. Then, at a rock ledge, the road sloped down to a corner.

We rounded the curve. A valley spread out before me.

"What do you see? Do you see anything in particular?"

"I see fields, mountains, and maybe a road. Is something else there?"

"That's the military facility."

I scrutinized the valley and mountainside. I saw nothing. *If flying over this land looking for this base, it wouldn't be seen by friend or foe.*

France

I glanced at the ground by my feet. Again, pleasantly surprised by the flora, I asked, "Is this wild lavender?"

Terry confirmed, "It is."

On the return trip, I saw lavender everywhere. Once back at the car, I held my hand toward Dad. "Guess what's growing wild." Not waiting, I opened my hand. "Lavender!" I opened my other. "Rosemary too and Mistletoe!"

Dad informed me, "I also saw rosemary, and I saw a big insect. I walked over to look at it a second time, but it was gone. It was a nice Orthopteron, like a Morman Cricket or a Katydid."

I thought upon long ago times. At the tender age of six, my young heart was quite shocked when I discovered that my bug doctor father was not fixing the broken legs and wings of the insects he captured. Unlike the injured bird my sisters and I had found that he and my mother had helped nurse back to health, I found out that my father killed insects in cyanide and alcohol jars.

I got over that devistating realization quickly. I spent many enjoyable days helping my father collect Caddisfly larvae in creeks with cold, fast moving water. Many a night, with a plain jar and its lid, I relished plucking the insects I was instructed to collect from a white sheet with a light shining on it. The memories warmed my heart.

We piled into the car and went back to Terry's for sweet potato slices sprinkled with large grains of salt, rewarmed mutton, bread, and cheese.

After lunch, we tried to find the French Orthodox monastery, Saint Michel Du Var. Gisele had told us that they had recently finished painting it. Terry turned off the main road just past two giant clay jars that marked the entrance into a pottery facility. The stony ground beside the gravel road contained barely a grain of dirt. On the other side of the rain splotched window, grew field after field of three inch diameter grape vines with their young branches running along metal wires. At a snail's pace, we drove down the extremely primitive, rough, and stony road.

Provence

At its end, Dad offered his explanation, "You turned off the main road too soon."

With a ten-point maneuver, Terry turned the car around. We went back to the most recent divergence of roads. Then, to my surprise, we were taken deeper into the vineyard. At a sign with the words, 'propriété privée ne pas entrer,' Terry turned up the road.

I'm sure she knows what that sign said better than I, but I feel pretty sure that I understand those words. I cautioned, "I think that says private property. Don't enter."

"Power wires are going up this road. Somebody will be there to ask which way."

Somebody who doesn't want us to be here!

Carefully navigating over large stones, Terry continued up the private road. We passed a shed then saw a house not much farther ahead. As Terry attempted to round the loop that would point us back out, a woman ran from her house. Terry exited the car. In furious French, the woman scolded her.

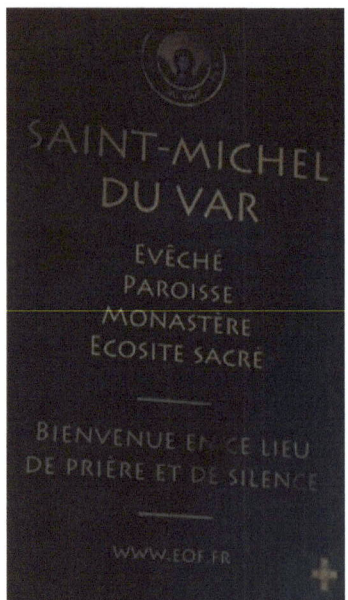

After Terry had explained our plight, the woman calmed and told her which way to go. Terry returned to the car. "She says this happens all the time. She wishes the church would put up a sign at her road that notified the people it was not the way to the church."

We slowly backtracked. At the main road, Terry turned left. We immediately saw the sign that marked the correct road. A short way in, we came to the parking lot. Just beyond, we saw an archway. Carol remarked, "This is it."

Across a pond, we saw the edge of the monastery.

France

We walked up a dirt path to the church. In front, stood a replica of a boat. I attemped to read the sign written in French. *Wow! A boat just like this one brought Mary Magdalene, Martha, and Lazarus to France. I always wondered what happened to them. That was a long way to come in such a small boat. They had to have been very brave. Then again, after watching the gruesome death of Jesus, I guess nothing would be anywhere close to that horrible.*

The construction of this modern day monastery was begun in 2005. The painting of the church's interior was completed ten years later in 2015. The Russian design artist, who was also the painter, currently lives with his family in Tourtour. Tourtour is the village close to the home of Terry.

Provence

A tiny nun in a habit, one of the six women who live at the monastery, explained the paintings and Terry translated. The nun spoke about the artwork that represented creation, Noah's ark and the flood, and the birth and death of Christ. "You cannot make a likeness of the Father. He is the star in the ceiling." She pointed above. "These waves are the Holy Spirit coming down and sitting as tongues of fire over the Apostles." After allowing us a few minutes to take in the painting, she led us to the beautiful painting of the archangel Michel commanding the army of heaven to cast out the serpent, Lucifer. We looked at Christ watching over his sheep, the wise men visiting the Holy Family in Egypt, and many others.

France

After we left Saint Michel Du Var Monastery, we traveled to Tourtour. There, we stopped at the Church of Tourtour, which overlooked the village and a large portion of the valley.

Provence

I went into the church. Immediately inside, I passed a small doorway that opened to a circular stairwell. Next, I came to an alcove with a painting of their patron, the Arch Bishop of Paris; Saint Denis. The art told the story of a miracle attributed to Saint Denis. Two young men were brutally murdered in Tourtour. After their death, in a dream, they came to a woman and told her that they were trapped in Hell and the only way they could escape their torment was if Arch Bishop Denis said a mass for them. Two devoted women in the congregation prayed that the Bishop would do so. Denis did indeed say a mass for them. The two souls again came to the woman who they had first contacted and let her know that they had been set free and were in Heaven.

Around a corner to the right of the painting, I discovered a tunnel to a closed door. At the front of the small, dimly lit church, was the altar area, with a slender stained glass window light, a statue of the Virgin Mary and Child, Christ on a cross, and statues of various saint behind bars.

All this art is probably just like God would have seemed to many of the common folks back then; blurry and out of reach behind the altar and the Latin language.The bishop also inaccesible to the point where they felt they had to pray to get the man to even say a mass.That's why they have him behind bars. Then again, it's probably just so current day people can't steal the statues. They're probably valuable art.

France

Continuing left, situated in another alcove, I encounter a rack of candles and a statue of the Virgin Mary. I passed a picture of Christ's face. Next, I came to a statue of Saint Antoine de Padoue with candles one can light if needing his help to find something lost.

At the rear of the church, an abstract painting of the Lord's supper on the wall below the balcony. Unfortunately, the lighting prevented me from being able to take a picture of the interesting blue painting in which the faces had been abstracted into pyramids.

Past the door through which I had entered the church, hung a painting of a plaque with the names of the men of Tourtour who died in World War I.

I returned to the stairwell, which was glowing with light. Up the stairs I went, my footsteps echoing in the stone passageway. Halfway up, I peeked through an open door at the top of a set of modern wooden steps.

That looks like a storage area. I saw workmen downstairs. Best to keep out.

Round and round I ascended into the darkness beyond the light from a tiny window.

Provence

Set in the stone wall of the balcony, a lovely circular window allowed light into the church. I turned and looked down at the beautiful simplicity of the altar area then carefully made my way down the much-too-narrow steps that faded away to nothing at the inner circle.

Once on the main floor, I exited the church into the clear, very cold air. As the bells tolled, I turned to the church and snapped a farewell picture. I hurried to the car and waited with my parents.

France

At Terry's house, we ate duck soup with angel hair pasta, bread, cheese, and grapes. With dinner, Terry served Communard, which is red wine mixed with Crème de Cassis, the blackcurrant liqueur.

Terry told the story of how the drink was invented. "One year, all the wine came out very bad. Nobody wanted to drink it. 'What will we do? We'll be ruined if we can't sell our wine.'

"They thought, and they thought. 'I know! Let us mix the wine with Crème de Cassis.'

"So they did. 'This is delicious,' the people said. Ever since people have drunk Communard. Kir is what we call Crème de Cassis mixed with rosé wine."

As it always does, the wine settled into my brain. I felt it putting me to sleep, so I snuggled under my warm comforter and was soon asleep.

Provence

The Storm

5:30 am and I'm wide awake. I'll get up and type my notes.

I did so until 8 am when I heard Carol ask, "Lisa, will you come help me?"

"Of course." I went into the bathroom.

"This water won't turn on."

Not again! I turned the knobs. Water flowed. *Hmm. I don't know.* After eating yogurt and toast with lavender honey, I again typed my notes until it was time to go.

Terry instructed us, "I'll pick you up on the road again."

I stood in the drizzle and watched Terry attempt to make the curve out of her garage into the driveway.

Crunch.

That's not good. Poor tree. Terry pulled back into the garage then tried again. *Still too far to the right.* After a few attempts to make the curve, Terry reversed up the drive. Dad, Carol, and I got in. Off we went. All around us, puddles filled the low ground. The olive groves appeared to rise out of lakes. Unavoidably, Terry swerved around curves and cars all the way to the village. In Aups, a strong, cold wind accosted us. We stood beside a large Sycamore tree and watched Magpies playing in the wind.

Terry parked down the road then rejoined us. "I'll meet you in front of the church at 1:30." She hurried away.

The rain picked up. I pointed. "Let's try the visitor's center."

Stopping every few minutes for Dad to get his breath, we hurried as fast as he could go. We got my father safely out of the rain and wind and into a place with chairs and interesting displays. Carol asked the young lady behind the desk. "Can you make change for a twenty?"

"No, but you could try the post office. They might."

I remembered where the post office was located. Carol and I went back into the rainy wind. We walked the narrow road past cobblestone side lanes, hemmed in by row houses. In the post office, Carol was told, "If you buy stamps, I can make change." Carol declined.

I suggested, "Let's go to the meat store and see if I can get the ground beef." In the gusting wind, we searched for the butcher shop. Up and on the other side of the road, we finally found it.

Carol instructed, "Make sure you can use your card."

Good plan. I held up my credit card. The lady nodded her head as she ran the card of the customer before me. In French, Carol requested, "½ kilo of beef, ground."

Dark red beef, ground on the spot, extruded onto the butcher paper in the attendant's hand. I held the first ingredient for the Chili I wanted to make for Terry's birthday. *You can't get ground beef any better than this.*

Carol and I went in search of vegetables. Farther up the road, men folded tables. Beside them, sat crates of lettuce and other vegetables. I walked under the awning and picked up a yellow bell pepper. A man called out excitedly. Carol translated. "We can't buy it. They're closed."

France

The man's expression did not look kind. I put the pepper down and backed away. We continued up the road but found no vegetables. Soon, we saw no stores at all. We retraced our steps past the homes that bordered the cobblestones.

There in the wall, I saw it. "An ATM; maybe I can withdraw cash in Euros." I slid my card into the slot.

The words, 'Select your language,' displayed on the screen. I pressed 'English,' then saw, 'Enter your pin.'

I pressed the symbols on the screen. Nothing happened. Carol tried. Nothing happened. I glanced down. "Oh, here's an actual keyboard." I pressed the real buttons.

I was offered, 'Select your amount.'

"Everything costs a lot. How much do you think I should get?" I asked my stepmother.

"I don't know," she replied.

I don't want any leftover money, but I don't know when I'll be able to get more. I guess it's better to have too much. I pressed the 200.00 button.

The machine displayed the question, 'Do you want a receipt?'

I selected, 'Yes.'

'Remove your card. Your money will be dispensed below.'

I don't want the money to blow away. I pulled my card and shoved it into my change purse. The receipt fed out. *Oh no. I'm sure to miss the money.* I jerked the paper, crammed it into my purse, and then quickly pinched my fingers around the money exiting the slot. With my money safely under control in the gusting wind, I added it to my purse of currently useless American dollars. "At least I've accomplished two objectives."

"Let's check on your father."

"All right." I too desired to make sure Dad was still out of the weather. Also, I didn't want to continue to wander in the worsening storm. Back at the tourist center, we found Dad looking at a model of Provence. Carol and I joined him. Together, we looked at products made of Truffles. For 44.00 € a small can of black truffles could be had, or one could purchase mustard with Truffles for only 7.00 €. Other products were also available.

"Are you getting some?" I asked.

"I'm thinking about it."

The attendant locked the door to the far room. I knew she spoke English. "Are you closing?"

"At 12:30."

I looked at my phone. "It's 12:29." *We're losing our safe haven. I don't want to stand in this storm for an hour, and I'm sure not letting Dad do that.* "Maybe the church is open."

41

Provence

My stepmother hurried around the corner and checked. "It's not open."

"Yes, they are." I told her, "I see the open door."

"The outer are but not the inner."

I walked down the steps and tried the knob. *I don't read French. 'Entre', however, looks like the right word.* I followed the arrow to a small side door set in the large locked door. I pushed. "It's open. Come on."

I quickly snapped photos of the inside of the ornate church. "I know where the lady said the store is located. Dad, we'll be right back. Come on, Carol, I need you." Once more in the storm, Carol and I walked up a different road. "I think that's it." We went inside Boucherie Hughes. *We have indeed found the store we need.* Carol went searching for the items she wanted while I placed canned kidney beans, tomato paste, tomato sauce, and cayenne pepper into my arm. I looked for the other items I wanted. *Drat. The fresh vegetables are outside. I don't want anybody to think I'm trying to steal these if I walk out the door with them, and Carol is at the cooler.* I put my items on the counter and slipped outside to look for bell peppers. I saw none, and it had gotten really cold. I returned to the warmth. The storeowner had come to the front and was already ringing up the items I had placed in front of the register.

"Do you speak English?" I asked.

"No."

"Bell peppers?"

He shrugged his shoulders. I pulled out my phone and typed bell peppers in the search bar. Soon, I had the image. I turned my phone toward the man. "Bell pepper."

"No."

Oh well, I guess I can make chili without bell peppers. I saw the amount on the register display; 8,86 €. I knew Carol's main objective. I handed the man a fifty-euro note. *This way I can make change for Carol.* The man gave me my change then went outside to get and bring in his vegetables. I started toward the rear of the store, "The store is closing," I informed my stepmother.

She remained at the cooler. The approaching vegetable rack prevented me from exiting via my path of ingress. I continued to the rear. "Make your selection. You're in the man's way." The large metal frame drew nearer. I turned to the only other aisle. My stepmother selected a container of goat cheese then followed me.

France

I remembered that Terry had said she wanted potatoes. I plucked four from the shelf as the man went past. He deposited the vegetables in front of the open cooler then returned to the register. I paid for the potatoes then moved out of the way. I looked at the items on the end shelf as Carol handed the man her cheese. *Granola bars. I've felt hungry every night. I hope he'll keep selling.* I grabbed a box and placed it on the counter. To my delight, he rang me up, took my 20, and returned more change.

We loaded our purchases beside the ground beef in the bag I had brought from Terry's then headed back to the church. So far, we had progressively stayed ahead of the closing schedule of the various establishments. At the church, where we were to meet Terry, Dad stood in the outside vestibule.

"Why are you out here?" I asked.

"They closed."

This time I was worried. We weren't in a good situation. The rain was significant. The wind was too, and Terry's return was more than half an hour away. I didn't know how much longer the small space outside the inner door would be open and there weren't any seats there either. *Where will we go?* On the other side of the traffic circle, I saw a plastic-surrounded overhang. "The café looks open." I crossed the street and tried the door. *Open. Thank you, God.*

I gripped the light plastic door, hoping the wind didn't rip it off. I also made sure it fastened when I pulled it closed. I followed Dad up the stairs into what was no more than a large room. On the right, the long bar was devoid of seats. Two four-seat-tables were positioned to the counter's left. Long tables filled the space beyond the bar. A couple occupied the first of the smaller tables. Two groups of men filled the rear tables.

My stepmother pulled out one of the four chairs at the only open table. "I guess we should order something."

The waitress made expresso at the coffee machine below a decorated wild boar head and a painting of a ship sailing on an ocean in a suitcase.

At the counter, the tap handles were labeled: Vino Rouge, Vino Rosé, I don't know, I don't know, Leffe. Dad and I got settled in. The lady carried two tiny cups to the table where one of the men rolled out a two-foot by foot-and-a-half woven matt. He pulled a worn deck of cards from his pocket and then took his brew of warm liquid energy. The waitress deposited the other cup on the table.

Provence

She arrived at our table and did what a French waitress would do. She spoke French words. It seemed reasonable to believe she had asked what we wanted. Dad replied, "Vino Rosé."

The order taker looked at Carol, who said, "Leffe."

The woman repeated, "Leffe," – pronounced differently than Carol had said the word.

My turn. "Leffe," I tried to say the word correctly. I'm sure I mangled it anyway.

"That's beer," Carol remarked.

The waitress remained where she stood.

"I know."

"You don't drink beer. I've never seen you drink beer."

I certainly have taken a swallow or two of my husband's beer while sitting in my parent's living room, but it is true that beer is not my beverage of choice. "I usually don't drink any kind of alcohol, but I've tasted Leffe. I know what I'll get."

The waitress asked, "Leffe?"

"Leffe," I confirmed my order.

Out of the wind and rain, I sipped my beer as my parents sampled their drinks. As we waited for Terry, I watched the men at the tables behind us. I told my parents, "I'm glad I'm here to see real French life."

One gentleman after another entered the bar and joined the men playing cards. Obviously enjoying the show, they cheered on the two players. One of the competitors nonchalantly leaned back in his chair. He slung his card onto the mat. I assumed he said, *Ha Ha!* in his head as he revealed the winning card.

Carol looked out the side door. "It sure is bad out there."

Drawing near to 1:30, I spoke up. "I guess we'll have to go out so Terry can find us."

"Let me finish my beer." My stepmother took another swallow.

Suddenly, Terry's smiling face appeared inside the room.

"I'm glad you found us!" I exclaimed.

"This is pretty much the only place to be right now. Let's wait and see if the rain lets up." As the storm grew worse, Terry flipped through the bar copy of the local paper. After perusing the news, she picked up the red umbrella. "I don't think the weather is going to get better. I'll get the car." She bravely made her way through the blowing rain.

We paid for our drinks then stood under the plastic enclosed awning, hammered by the rain. In the lane for traffic going the other way, Terry pulled up to the front of the Café. As we had when we had been at the market, we once again blocked traffic in Aups. Out of the weather, people sat in their cars and honked their horns until they saw Dad struggling to get into the car in the pouring rain. The very intelligent French people realized why Terry was there and stopped honking. *That wouldn't have happened back home. People there wouldn't have cared.*

France

Finally all inside, Terry slowly and carefully backed out of the traffic circle. With the way cleared, the other travelers shot past. Terry gave every one of them a wave of thanks.

Dad instructed Terry, "Go slow. With this much rain, the roads are going to be very dangerous."

Terry drove the same way she had on every other trip. Unable to keep ourselves from doing so, my stepmother gasped in fear, and I kept a death grip on the door armrest.

Back at the house, we remained in the car until we were safely inside the garage. When again in dry clothes, we joined at the table. While the storm raged on the other side of the glass doors, we ate tasty grapes along with sandwiches of Prosciutto ham, Swiss cheese, and dressing.

Lightning lit up the sky. The thunder crashed only a second later. Terry jumped up from the table. "I need to unplug the satellite receiver." She dashed across the room as the wind screamed ferociously and quarter-inch hail bounced off the porch railing.

Unable to activate my camera before the hail had stopped, I consoled myself by taking a picture of the ice balls on the porch outside the kitchen door.

Before we retired from the table, another round of hail pounded the mountain. While the others napped, I recorded this tale of my experiences in France. At 6:30 pm, I walked into the living room. My parents sat at the table reading. Terry lay on the couch doing the same. I interrupted them to ask for what I needed: the name of the type of bug Dad had observed and an explanation of the pictures and statues in the Church of Tourtour.

Finally, Terry remarked, "Carol, you're not hungry yet are you?"

"To tell you the truth, I'm thinking about going to bed," Carol replied.

"It's too early, and I have a special treat for tonight." Terry went into the kitchen. She returned and placed a can on the table. We examined the offering then waited for the meal of spiral pasta and Black Truffle sauce.

We ate Truffle sauce as Terry regaled us with the story of Saint Denis, the patron saint not only of Tourtour, of all of France. Saint Denis, whose likeness I had seen in the church at Tourtour, was the Bishop of Paris in the third century. He was beheaded, becoming a martyr for his faith. According to Catholic legend, the decapitated bishop picked up his head and walked while preaching a sermon on repentance.

We also spoke about Saint Asaph, who has a street named after him back home in Alexandria, Virginia. While still young, Asaph had served Saint Kentigern. Kentigern had asked Asaph to bring a burning branch to start a fire. Instead, Asaph brought live coals in his apron without any harm.

As I retired to my bed, the rain, wind, and hail pounded the land. I lay under the covers and thought about the delicate flavor of the Truffle sauce. It was nice but had left me disappointed. Truffles did not taste as awesome as I had anticipated. Still, it was very generous of Terry to serve us such an expensive dish, and now I can say that I have eaten a Truffle.

Provence

All Saints Day

We took the road to Aups passed Château de Turenne. Its occupants reigned over the olive trees surrounding the castle and the business empire the olives generated. This morning, as we crunched over rocks washed into the road by the heavy rains, the ground under the olive trees was visible. Terry informed us, "There was damage in Nice from the rain and the waves of the sea. But not to worry; everything will be good when you get there." We traveled past trees, full of olives that I could have reached from the road. Having already been told that olives are not ripe until January, and more importantly being in a speeding car, I didn't attempt to pluck any.

Just outside of Aups, unable to exit through the grates, the water had become trapped between high walls of stone. Ahead, a car barreled down on us. A man with no place to exit stood in the road raking leaves and rocks from the drain. We screeched to a halt in the narrow lane. Seemingly with no concern, the car coming toward us sped past. Terry drove around the man, still raking away with no apparent knowledge that he had almost been squashed like a bug on the road.

We rounded the circle and continued past the Hunter's Café where we had taken refuge the previous day. Today is All Saint's Day. Everything is closed, luckily except the gasoline pumps still running for credit card purchases. I looked at the sign. 1,539 € per liter. *Over six dollars a gallon.* Again, I thought *that's a lot.*

We exited the lot with a tank of gas, again purchased by my father. We took the road to Fox Amphoux. Along the way, I saw something. "Terry, what's that?"

"It's a small shrine. There are many in France. Each holds a statue of a saint. In the past, people on a pilgrimage used them as landmarks."

"They were on a pilgrimage? To where?"

"Different places. They traveled on foot all across Europe."

Not much further along, Terry informed us, "Starting today, many people will be out looking for mushrooms."

"What kind?" I asked.

"Small yellow or gray ones. I don't know what they're named." Terry pointed at a cluster of yellow buildings sitting on top of a tall hill to our left. "That is where we are going."

One tight hairpin curve after the other, we drove back and forth up a hill. We parked just outside of Fox Amphoux. "That is the tree," our hostess informed us. A Hackberry stood in the churchyard ahead. Planted in 1550, its branches, that have grown as big as a regular sized tree, were supported by wires running from one limb to another. The branches rose above the main trunk, so large it blocked my view of our car behind it.

France

The church's high bell tower chimed 12, followed by a short series of chimes a few minutes later. We entered the church with walls several feet thick. The light that entered from the stained glass window turned the stones to a beautiful lavender.

Alcoves held statues of Saint Teresa and Saint Joseph. Hanging in the altar area was a wooden crucifix. I took it all in then did an about face and ascended the stairs that rose to a small balcony at the rear of the church. I stated my opinion. "This church could have been used as a fort."

We exited the church. "I'm sure it would have been," Dad replied.

"I want to take you to the tower." Terry led me up the hill.

I followed under an archway with an overhead plaque. "Does that sign say 'to the prison'?"

"Yes."

I'm not sure if the tower was part of the prison, but we entered its stairwell. Terry pressed the elevator button. The door did not open. "You go." Terry pointed at a stairwell.

I started up. *I'll count the stairs. No, that may discourage me from continuing.* I climbed round and round up several flights of stairs. High above the world, I stepped into the wind that swept over the village. The entire landscape was visible in every direction. *Truly the perfect fort! They would have been able to see an approaching enemy long before anybody arrived. If they rang the bell, all the villagers would've had plenty of time to get safely into the church.*

Provence

I videoed as I walked the narrow path around the square summit. *Drat! My phone died.* I pulled my battery pack from my hip pouch and then searched for the small adaptor I needed to attach it to my phone. Having just found and removed it from its protective bag, I heard, "Lisa, come on down."

"Just a minute, my phone died. I'm hooking up my spare battery." I plugged in the cable then impatiently waited for my phone to boot up. *Finally!* I quickly snapped photos of the information plaques.

Terry called again, "Lisa, come down!"

I leaned over the edge. Terry stood in the courtyard below, looking my way.

"Coming!" I replied. Then, so I didn't fall and break my neck, I carefully made my way down the stairs.

France

Snapping photos of the constricted lanes between the homes, I walked past the car to the large information plaque. With Dad and Carol, Terry pulled up in the car. Carol got out and read the information written in French. The first paragraph of which had also been written in English. I can put the information in the computer and translate the French portion later. Back in the car, Dad buckled his seat belt. "Let's find a place to eat lunch."

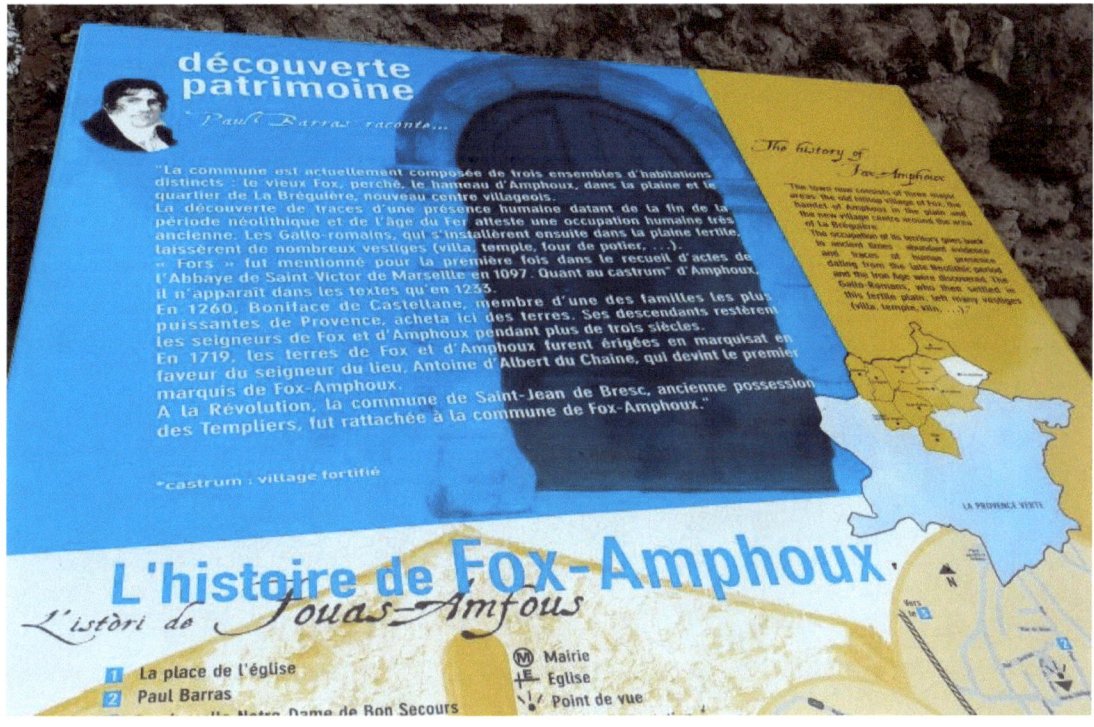

"I know just the place. It's on the way to Riez." Terry put her Peugeot into drive.

Much farther along the winding road, I saw Lac de Saint Croix far below on our left. We curved back and forth all the way down the mountain to the river running into the lake. Not the beautiful teal of my last visit, the river ran brown and high, spilling over its banks onto the floodplain. In the water, several canoes moved upstream.

Provence

Still high above the lake, Terry pulled into a small parking lot at the edge of a cliff in Quinson. "We're here. They serve wild meat that hunters have killed." Across the road, nestled into the cliff side, was Chez Kinou.

In the back left corner of the restaurant, part of the mountain protruded inside. A large cooking pot hung in a hollow space in the rock. "I wonder if people actually cooked there."

France

I took a picture then sat at the table and looked at the menu I couldn't read.

Terry translated, "This meal you can pick from green salad, pâté of wild rabbit, or pâté of wild boar, or wild bird, and also pick wild boar, wild bird, or wild rabbit cooked roasted, and a dessert too."

"I would like to have pâté of wild rabbit, the main dish of wild boar, and what are the dessert choices?"

Carol thought that was wrong. "Not all those things. You have to pick between them."

"You get to pick from each of the two groups," Terry informed us.

The waitress arrived and explained in French, "You are both wrong. You get a salad, and you pick one pâté, and you also get the main dish of your choice and for dessert, I will bring you a list later."

I pointed to what Terry had told me were the choices I wanted. Dad ordered then Carol and Terry. As we waited for our meals, I took in the decorations that surrounded us. Beside the hearth, a fox with a magpie in its mouth popped its head out from a hollow log. Animal heads on plaques hung on the wall. A stuffed baby pig had been placed on a mantel. Not far over, a weasel that had met its demise appeared to slink over a mess of items on a shelf.

My gaze riveted on small monsters perched above the teapots. "What are those?" I walked across the room. *Fish heads! Those are the ugliest things I've ever seen!*

I returned to our table as Dad remarked, "I don't like it when people bring their crying babies into a concert or a nice restaurant."

Since Dad had tempted Murphy into action, a couple walked up to the door with a toddler in a backpack. "People just outside the door have a baby in their backpack," I informed my father.

The couple remained outside the door for several minutes. "Maybe they're not coming in."

Provence

A second couple arrived with their own young child on his father's back. Together, they came in and removed their offspring from their confinement. The children followed each other to the door then behind the counter. As their fathers chased them, the mothers looked at their smartphones.

Terry related a short tale, "I was at a restaurant in Austria, and there was a screaming child. I went over and said," in a sharp tone Terry continued her story, "'Stop screaming!' and the child did so."

While we waited for our food, another couple with a toddler and a large family with children arrived.

I guess French Murphy really socks it to you. You guessed it; four children started crying. Terry got up and walked to a set of parents and their child.

I think it's rude to tell parents to make their child be quiet. I'm sure they would if it was possible. In my opinion, people with children have the right to partake of a meal in a restaurant.

Terry spoke to the child as his mother held him. His wide-eyed expression, to me, said, 'Why are you speaking to me, and are you going to bite my head off?' Soon, however, the child happily smiled at Terry.

She walked to the next couple and repeated the procedure. After speaking with all the families with young children, Terry rejoined us at our table, in a room of silent children. I don't know what she said, but I saw that she had completed her rounds with a smile and nobody seemed offended.

Our salads arrived along with Carol's plate of thinly sliced meats. I sampled the pâté. Not bad. The circle of roasted rabbit tasted strongly of thyme. The dressing on the salad was quite tangy but also acceptable.

When we had finished our salads, the waitress replaced the plates with clean ones then carried over a large white chafing dish. She pointed to Dad and me and then held out a dish. I took it. "I think this is the wild boar for both of us."

I placed the container on the table between us. The young lady returned with bowls of spaghetti noodles for Dad and me. She came back again with Terry's roasted bird and Carol's leg of chicken, both with parsley potatoes.

I spooned out four chunks of meat and drenched my noodles with wine and bay leaf sauce. "Terry, what kind of bird are you eating?" I asked.

After much discussion about the habits of the bird, Dad decided it must be a type of small pheasant. I punched it into my phone and showed Terry the picture. Still seeming unsure, she agreed it was the bird.

Dad took a bite of boar meat. "This is so tender; it falls apart. They must have cooked it a long time."

Not liking large chunks of food, I easily knocked my pieces apart then sampled the fare. "The flavor of the wine sauce rendered the pig meat's flavor undecipherable, but it tasted good."

France

By the time I was at the bottom of my noodles, the children were again crying. Pausing at our table only long enough to deposit a plaque listing the deserts, the waitress hurried past. Terry explained the choices. "This one is a pastry with piñon nuts. This is lemon with beaten egg whites on top. This is custard with egg whites in milk sauce…."

Terry attempted to wave the blonde-haired waitress over. Seen only by me, the waitress acknowledged the summons but continued to the bar to make an espresso. After a few minutes of fiddling with the machine, she went into the kitchen. Terry again went to the crying children. A young man in an apron, who I assume was the chef, returned with the waitress. He worked on the machine as the waitress arrived with her notepad. "Terry," I called out.

Terry did not turn. Dad ordered, "Crème Brûlée."

Terry and I had decided that we would share two desserts. I would order the pastry with the piñon nuts, and she would order sorbet. I didn't, however, know which flavor. "Terry!"

Carol stated her choice, "Lemon Meringue."

"Terry!" I pointed to the Tarte aux Pignons, "and sorbet for…" I called out more forcefully, "TERRY!"

The waitress glared across the room. Terry turned, hurried across the once again quiet restaurant, and named the flavors she wanted.

Having finally gotten the Espresso machine working, the chef disappeared into the kitchen. I hoped to quickly prepare our desserts.

The Crème Brûlée arrived with no flames. On Carol's lemon pie, a long string of meringue had been squeezed from a pastry bag back and forth across the top and then toasted. My pastry was topped with a shiny, sugary, piñon nut glaze. Terry's dessert glass was filled with a small scoop of lemon sorbet and another of Cassis. She placed half of each scoop of very tart sorbet on my plate.

I cut the pastry wedge in half. Alternating between the frozen,

tart Sorbet and the warm, sweet pastry, I consumed my desert.

Two hours after our arrival, we braved the rain and hurried back to the car. Dad wedged himself through the door. "I don't think we have time to go to Riez."

"We have time." Terry shifted into reverse.

Carol asked, "Aren't we supposed to be in Tourtour by five."

I'm keeping my mouth shut. I'll go where ever I'm taken and be happy.

Terry replied, "Let me worry about the time."

Provence

In Reiz, Terry pointed. "There's the Baptistery." We walked to a square building. Terry went down the stairs and tried the door. "It's locked, but you can see inside. Come see."

I joined Terry and attempted to see into the darkened interior.

That would have been a tight fit. It must have been hard to dunk a person in that little hole. With my phone lens between the links of the fence inside the door, I snapped a shot of the baptistery pool. I could look at the ceiling, but my phone couldn't take a photograph at that angle.

Terry called, "Carol, come look. It's worth it."

Carol came down the stairs. "I saw snails and a yellow flower." She pointed. We ascended to leave but paused to look at a flower growing out of the stairs and some small white snails beside a tree.

I had noticed an excavation across the road. "Let's go over there." I tried to determine if I was looking at ruins being excavated or a new structure being built. The stone joints looked tight from where I stood.

I sloshed through ground water to the orange fence that kept me away from the structure. Still not able to get close enough to determine if the structure was old or new, I took several pictures for analysis. Later, I was told it was indeed a Roman excavation.

France

Carol noticed a large, unusually shaped boulder. "Is this natural?"

I stepped into a puddle to circle the object. "I don't think so. It looks carved."

Terry pointed through the trees. "Over there are the Roman ruins." I zoomed my lens and pressed the button. "Can we drive over?"

"No."

Drat! I wish I had been able to touch something the Romans built.

To get home by five, we hurried away on a high mountain road with only a guardrail to prevent us from meeting splattered ends. We wound down the mountain past Saint Croix, Lac de Saint Croix, fields of harvested lavender with short sunflowers around their edges, and wheat silos.

Provence

We arrived home minutes before five. Dad and Carol decided to stay home. Terry and I hurried to the church in Tourtour for the All Saints Day mass. That rainy night, we slipped into the church as the priest spoke blessings in the dark graveyard then entered the church alone. Terry whispered, "Everybody who had been in the graveyard must have left. Nobody attends church anymore. It's very sad."

"I know a pastor who has a service even if nobody comes. He says he worships God no matter what."

Terry replied, "Where two or more are gathered in his name, He is in the midst of them."

I sat beside Terry in the very plain church and admired the beautiful stonework of the half dome before me. I contemplated how the stones must be shaped for them to not fall in. With only ten people in the pews, the priest began the service. I didn't know what was being said, until I recognized the melody of the doxology. When they sang hallelujah, Gloria in excelsis Deo, I softly added my voice to almost a millennia of voices that have worshiped God inside the stone structure put together in 1038.

Terry went forward and spoke the first reading.

Afterward, the priest consecrated the communion bread and wine. He drank the wine and ate a fourth of a wafer of bread then offered the people a small round wafer. I went forward and received one. More songs were sung. The priest sat in a chair at the side for a moment of silence. I assumed for people to raise the names of their loved ones who had departed. I silently thought my list.

Another woman read a second Bible passage.

A man walked to the front and read a liturgical passage to which the congregation responded. In the end, I was glad to have worshipped my God. Even though I do not know the language, I understood the spirit of worship.

As we drove home, I asked, "Are there other churches in Tourtour?"

"Not here, and almost all of the churches in France are Catholic, but there are some protestant, and some synagogues, and mosques."

"As long as they believe that Jesus Christ is God born of the Virgin Mary, that He led a perfect life and died to save us from our sins, and that He was resurrected on the third day and now sits at the right hand of God as our intercessor; the rest of the service around it is man-designed. It doesn't matter what form it takes. The church should also believe and preach that the Bible was written by man under the inspiration of God and is inerrant. I know if he didn't forgive us that there would be no hope for me. I don't think right or act right. I'm not saying I'm a murderer or anything like that, but I know I'm a long way from right. If I weren't covered in the righteousness of Christ, I would not be going to Heaven."

As we drove into her garage, Terry replied, "Yes, He died to help us."

France

Tourtour

Today is Terry's birthday. I want to prepare her chili for lunch. Terry sat at the breakfast table. "Will you stay home this morning and prepare the chili? Your parents and I will go into Tourtour this morning while I go for my hair appointment. I'll take you back to Tourtour in the afternoon when I take my mail to town."

"Of course I will."

After we cleared the table, I cut onions. I pushed the onions off the cutting board into the pot with the ground beef then attempted to turn on the stove. I looked at the knobs and buttons. *Looks like this one.* I turned the knob and waited for the eyelet to heat up. I tapped my finger on the surface. *Still stone cold.* I looked at the two symbols on the stove surface; one a line and one a zero. I pressed the line. A light came on. *Ah ha!* I removed my finger. The light went off. *How do I make it stay on?* After several minutes of unsuccessful maneuvers, I gave up. "Terry, will you show me how to use your stove?"

Once I had the beef and onions cooking, the others went to town. I added oil to the pot, opened the cans, and then added the beans and tomato sauce. I punctured the foil seal of a tube then squeezed out a glob of tomato concentrate. I need to turn this down. As I fiddled with the knobs, the conglomeration scorched at the bottom. *Drat! Still too hot! How do I turn this down?*

I moved the pot off the burner. Quickly, leaving quite a bit in the pot so as to not scoop out any of the burnt flavor, I spooned the chili off the top and into a second pot. I sampled the salvaged chili. *Wonderful, it doesn't taste burnt at all.* I retrieved a gallon sized Ziploc bag from my luggage, scraped the ruined food inside, sealed it closed, and then deposited it under the trash already in the container. *Nobody should find it there.*

I figured out how to adjust the stove to the lowest setting and again tried to successfully cook the remainder of the chili. After several minutes of careful attention and stirring, I turned the heat off and placed the lid over the top.

I needed to reduce my level of stress, so I ran water in the tub, and took a relaxing bath in the skinny tub. With soothed nerves, I closed the wooden window shutters and then climbed back into bed in the darkened room. After a long nap, I woke, just before Terry unlocked the door.

After everybody enjoyed the chili, Terry worked diligently to prepare her papers for mailing. I rode to Tourtour; a village nestled in with the rocks of the mountains.

Provence

Terry zipped into a parking spot next to a manikin propped under a large tree. She jumped out of the car. "The post is picked up at 3:30. We barely have time to get there."

We hurried around the castle that had been converted into the town hall, the center for tourism, and post office. Terry held out her flat.

"The post leaves at 3," the clerk took her mail, "But you're in luck; the man hasn't arrived yet." With her package safely in the system, Terry led us into the depths of Tourtour.

We stood outside a shop with a sign over the door that read, 'Curios'.

In the street, we looked at small metal bird sculptures and one of a hedgehog. I stepped into the store and slipped through the tight spaces between the racks of clothes that filled the front room and the room beyond. I stopped at a table of necklaces, bracelets, and earrings. *These look pretty.* I examined a set of black and silver teardrop earrings. *28 Euros! I'll look into all the shops before I decide where to spend my money.* I said to the woman, who probably didn't speak English, "I might come back for these after I look in all the shops."

We walked past the restaurants that surrounded the village's central fountain then under an arch into a narrow road that wound between rows of houses built around the boulders.

France

"Look at this!" My stepmother stood beside a fossil ammonite in the wall of the Museum of Fossils. I photographed her beside the proof that this land had once been under the ocean!

Yellow and tan homes, with visible timbers that served as the lintels over the door, nestled one to the next in wavy rows. Cobblestone paths, too narrow for cars, led to the opposite side of the village.

Clear spring water still flowed into a long stone trough that was once the public wash. In the wall that protected the area from the valley below, several long square posts protruded into the structure. Over the whole wash area, the terracotta roof was supported by hewn logs resting on ancient stone pillars. To the right of the structure, the original entry had been filled in with stones and mortar. We left what had once been a busy gathering spot of the women of Tourtour.

Provence

We traveled to the other castle situated across the village. This castle looked much older. With walls no longer dyed yellow with ochre from the quarries of France, it was rough and naked without plaster. We did not enter as it was closed for the season. We passed the giant ancient dwelling and then out of the village.

Just up the road, an ornate wrought-iron-cross stood on a stone pedestal.

Inscribed in the stone.
Mission
1855
LDMF

Through a hole in the broken glass window, I peeked at spider webs inside the tiny fifteen-foot square mission building.

France

We went back into the village and followed the small stream that ran through the concrete trough of the wash area. It emptied into a waterfall that cascaded over the high boulders at the upper village.

Past a blue door into the side of the mountain, I carefully made my way down the uneven steps beside the narrow waterfall.

Provence

In the lower part of the village, the stream was recaptured and routed to a building. Through a window at its rear, I peered at the water wheel that powered the still active local olive press.

Once again on the move, we circled the olive press to the back side of the fossil museum. Its tiny gift shop was stuffed with the shopkeeper and six tourists. I stood at the door and took a photo of the bone plesiosaur head. Three people exited the store. I maneuvered about the room being careful not to bump anything. I studied the geodes, crystals of amethyst and pyrite, shark teeth, and polished slices of ammonites. Also on display were pendants of amber and other shined up semi-precious minerals.

Everything in here is a trinket to collect dust on a shelf. I'd rather have the earrings. At least they have a practical use.

France

We wandered past a garden hanging over stone boulders between two homes. At a tight row of homes with only a narrow space between, Terry informed us. "This is the kind of path people did not walk at night. There was no light. Bandits would slit your throat and rob you."

Beautiful but deadly.

We trod on the patterned cobblestones that had prevented the path from becoming a muddy mess with all the rain of the preceding week. We rounded a corner then passed a lovely outside hearth beside another filled in archway.

Back at the Tourtour central fountain, I hurried to the 'Curios' shop, only to discover that it had closed. *I failed to follow my own advice. I didn't do what I could at the moment. Now, I've got no souvenir.*

Provence

At Terry's home, I smeared pork pâté on olive crackers. I then placed a slice of a tiny round pickle on the top of each. We covered other crackers with tangy goat cheese splashed with a green sprig of parsley. Terry filled bowls with pretzels, cashews, and mixed nuts. Bottles of rosé and red wine, along with a bottle of Cassis, were added to the table of hors-d'oeuvres. All was ready at the appointed hour, 6 pm. We waited. I tapped my foot impatiently. My clock reported 6:45 when the doorbell rang.

Just as I had heard her do when she answered her phone, Terry spoke what sounded like an English word before continuing her greeting in French. "Hello." I placed a kiss on both cheeks of each new arrival. Much to my happiness, several of Terry's guests spoke English as well as French. Of the two languages, my father and I speak only English, and a few of the lady guests spoke only French. Terry instructed each of us where to sit so that we could converse with the people beside us. Not knowing of another topic to bring up, I remarked to the lady seated at the end of the couch, "There's been so much rain since we arrived."

"In the last week, we've had half the amount of average rain for a whole year."

"Oh! I didn't know it was so much more than normal!" An hour of conversation about nothing of importance, and I was out of anything worth anybody's attention.

Terry brought plates of bite-size Quiche Loraine. *Something to do with my mouth that gives me an excuse to not talk instead of just being boring.* Inspiration hit me as I slowly ate the tasty morsel. Once consumed, I asked the handsome man to my right, "What do you do for a living?"

Intelligent conversation resumed. Before long, since he was retired, the man turned to the person on his other side. The pleasant woman to my left answered my father's question. "No, I grew up in Belgium. I came to France to study the language. Here, I met a man and fell in love. We married. I never went home. Such is love."

Nine in the evening arrived. Terry's guests departed. Some had a short drive to their home only a few streets away. Others had a long, nighttime drive on the narrow winding roads at the edge of mountain cliffs. As the wine had made me quite sleepy, I quickly prepared and was soon asleep.

France

La Bastide de Tourtour

Today, when we leave Terry's home, we will not come back. First thing to do after breakfast is to pack. I said farewell to the lovely house. I took a last, long look at the valley and the far away mountains once again visible after many days of rain then walked to the car designated to carry us to Nice. I loaded my luggage into the auto of Terry's sister, Solange, and Solange's husband, Alain.

There was one more scheduled pleasure to experience before we left Terry. Solange and Alain had invited us to a luncheon at La Bastide de Tourtour. On the lower side of Tourtour, we pulled up to the manor.

Its manicured lawns displayed statues amidst juniper trees shaped into spirals and a Kaki tree.

Terry called me over, "Show Annie how to take a picture with your phone. I want you to send me a picture of the six of us."

How am I going to do that? Annie and I don't speak the same language. I demonstrated without words.

Annie, complaining about something, pointed the camera and pressed the white button.

Terry looked. "We are not all here. Annie, take the picture again."

Provence

Annie again spoke words I did not understand. Solange explained, "She can't see anything."

I looked at my phone. "How did that happen? It's on the text messaging screen."

After a short conversation, Solange explained, "You received a text, and it took away the camera."

"Oh! All right. Annie, you get in the group. I'll take a picture and make sure everything is working correctly."

Solange passed the message. After a successful photo, I traded places. With the camera adjusted correctly, Annie took the perfect picture.

We made our way through the lovely building into a glassed-in porch where the sunlight streamed in.

Once again seated to Terry's specifications, I looked over the menu. *That's good!* I read the English translation just below each selection. The waiter returned with two bottles of water then stood by, ready to take our orders.

France

Terry spoke her request for the starter. The waiter turned to my father.

"Aren't you going to tell him the other things you want?" I asked.

"First, everybody tells what they want for the starter then everybody tells what they want for the main course and last what each of us want for dessert."

"Oh. I understand." I turned the menu around and pointed at the item I wanted. Once all three courses had been ordered, I picked up the bottle of fizzy water and held it over what I hoped was the correct glass. I whispered, "Terry, is this the right one?"

She nodded. I dispensed my water into the correct vessel as Terry placed one of each type of hors-d'oeuvres on a small plate. She handed it to me. I accepted my portion. I popped half a cherry tomato skewered together with a small ball of mozzarella cheese dipped in olive oil and spices. I nibbled the cheddar cheese wafer with a mound of tangy cream on top. The last looked like caviar. I was going to try it regardless of its make up, but I wanted to know what I was about to consume. "What's this one?" I asked.

"Ground olives and capers."

I smiled. *I'm so happy it's not fish eggs.* I bit off half the thin slice of crunchy bread with a pile of black on top. "All very tasty."

The waiter stood by my father with a bottle of rosé wine. He awaited acceptance of the offering.

Dad nodded his head. "I can't even smell, but this tastes fine."

All of our glasses received a half filling. I sipped my wine. Not being a sommelier, also known as a wine steward, it tasted just like what we have been drinking at Terry's home.

That's strange. Our waiter approached with a tray of white demitasse cups on teardrop-shaped saucers. Inside, a slightly green liquid with what looked like a tiny scoop of ice cream floating on top was placed before Terry. Words were spoken. Terry smiled. "This course is a gift from the chef. It's zucchini soup with truffle cream."

I carefully observed my friends. Once I had seen how they partook of the delicacy. I dipped in my small spoon and retrieved a taste of warm ground squash. *Lovely!* I stirred together the cream and soup, and then enjoyed one small spoonful after another.

Provence

All the tiny cups and their plates were removed before baskets of various types of bread were brought. I selected a skinny six-inch loaf that looked like herbed bread. Once again, the man serving us stood beside the table. He stated what he held. Alain raised his hand.

Oh no. I don't know the name of what I ordered.

Graciously saved by Terry, she pointed at me when the next dish was named. Centered in a glob of green then drowned in a white liquid, jiggled an orange oval sprinkled with white power. The colorful concoction with three solid yellow wedges of an unidentifiable matter was placed before me.

"What's that?" Dad asked.

"I guess these yellow things are the veal."

The waiter stated the name of the food on the next plate.

Terry corrected her previous error. "Oh, that's yours. I gave you mine."

I handed Terry the bowl containing what I guessed was an egg and received wafer thin slices of something brown surrounded by white under a sauce of tomato and spices.

Terry asked me, "Do you know that's veal?"

"Yes."

"It's from the head."

"You mean the brains?"

"No, just the head."

There can't be much in the way of meat on a baby cow head. Maybe that's why the slices are so thin.

I pulled a morsel to the side and piled it on one of the small toasted bread slices. *I hope it's good.* I cautiously placed the conglomeration into my mouth. Once again, a savory treat. I ate the whole serving minus a sample on half a toast that I gave my father and another that I gave to Carol.

To my left, Carol ate attractive slices of raw salmon shaped into fish. She cut off a head with its eye. "Would you like to try some salmon?"

I accepted the tasty sushi along with a serving of nugget from my father. Across the table, Annie, Solange, and Alain also ate nugget.

I looked at Terry's bowl. The ball in the center of her dish was indeed a raw egg yolk still in its thin membrane. Sipping bubbly water, I anticipated the entrée.

France

Once again, Terry identified my plate. Duck in orange sauce, basil roasted new potatoes, and vegetable medley. "This is a female duck," Terry informed me. I cut a bite of duck breast, swiped it through the sauce, and sampled. Tender and juicy, it delighted my taste buds. I savored the equally good potatoes and then the green beans, pea pods, and carrot slivers. I cut off a long slice of duck. "Dad, would you like to try some?"

He accepted the meat on my bread plate. "Sure. Would you like to try the veal?"

"No thank you. I had some for my starter."

Carol had also ordered duck. There was no reason to offer a sample.

The waiter approached with a tray of large parfait glasses. Chunks of orange colored passionfruit, nestled at the bottom of the clear glass, a thick layer of mousse of the same flavor, with a swirl of yellow around the raspberry perched at the top. One was set before Terry, Annie, my stepmother and me.

Across the table, Solange enjoyed coffee mouse while Alain ate fresh berries and my father dug into a tray of cheese.

The final offering. "Coffee?" the waiter asked.

Several accepted. Strong, highly caffeinated espresso is not something my heart can handle. I declined the coffee in favor of finishing the wine in my glass.

Overlooking the vast expanse of the valley below, an elegant and delicious lunch in the mountains of Provence France was an experience never to forget.

I kissed the cheek of Terry and thanked her for her gracious hosting over the preceding days. We left Terry and Annie behind.

As Solange and Alain whisked us away, I thanked them for the wonderful lunch.

Provence

We enjoyed an hour of smooth driving over country roads and in the fast traffic of the speed highway before Alain pulled up to the Ibis Hotel at Côte d'Azur, the coast of blue.

In Nice, after we had been checked in by a beautiful young lady with gorgeous eyelashes, we settled into our tiny room with three crammed together beds.

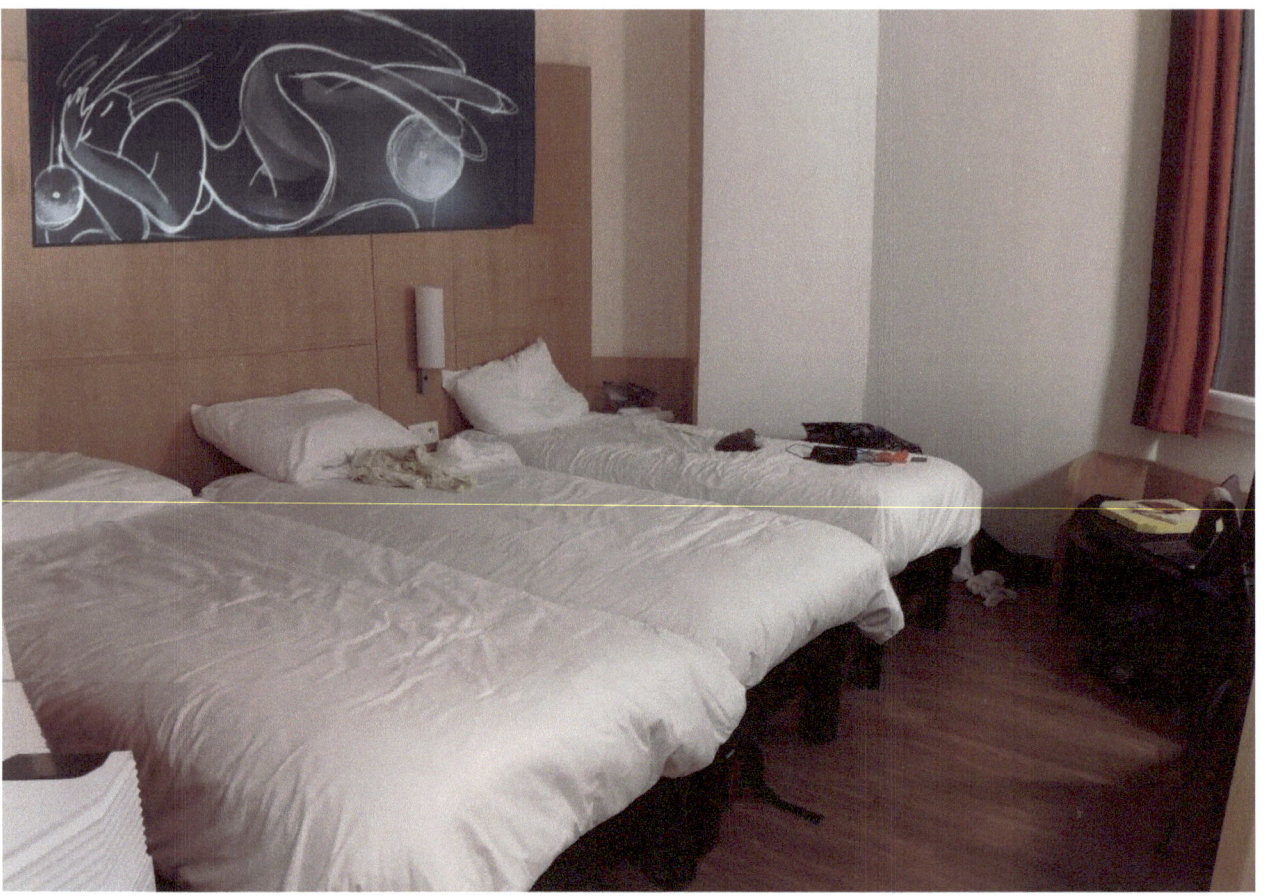

France

Côte d'Azur

One street inland from the beach of the French Riviera on the Mediterranean Sea, my parents and I sat in the breakfast area at the hotel. The buffet offerings were many: crepes, several types of bread that a person could place on the cutting board and hack off as much as they wanted, a citrus fruit medley, yogurts, sliced bread for toast, and jams. Timers, for people who want their eggs to be cooked to their exact specifications sat beside a crate of raw eggs, a vat of hot water, and cooking baskets. Figs, dates, raisins, and other dried fruits also sat on the breakfast bar. The always necessary coffee machine, bags of tea, and accouterments, were at the end of the long counter. Across the aisle, stood a fruit juice dispenser. I sliced off the top of my egg, cooked for exactly five minutes, then looked out the window. "Are we going to take a tour today?"

"I don't want to," my father informed me.

Carol echoed, "Nor do I."

Drat! Here I am on the Riviera, and I'm going to spend the day in a hotel room!

A flag passed. "The runners have arrived." I stood up. "Wow! Look how many!" I went outside and watched the masses of people running down Promenade Des Anglais beside the Mediterranean Sea. On and on they came from 7:30 am until 11 am, though only a straggler here or there after 9.

Planning to walk down Rue de France, My stepmother and I stepped into the street beside the hotel. "Oh, my word! Look at that car!" Parked outside a tall apartment building, sat a blue car. I looked up at the balconies displaying plants in terracotta pots. I looked at the dirt, broken jade plant, and chunks of broken terracotta far below.

Maybe the wind dislodged the pot and gravity brought it to its current location. But really, if the wind had blown that fiercely, the pot would've had a trajectory that wasn't straight down. More likely, the owner of the pot discovered the infidelity of a lover and retaliated. Still, it's better to smash a car than to attack a person, even a guilty one, but a broken heart doesn't often lend itself to intelligent decisions.

Provence

On to Musée Des Arts Asiatiques. I examined the plaque beside the gate. "The listed hours say it's open." I tried the gate. Despite the sign, the gate was locked. I stated my conclusion, "Probably closed for the race."

We returned to the hotel. Discouraged that I was not experiencing much of Nice, I asked the same young lady who had checked us in the afternoon before, "How hard is it to find a tour bus? For a person who doesn't speak French, is it safe to take a tour alone?"

"Perfectly safe, just go over one street," she pointed, "and take any train to the main station. The Office of Tourism is there. You can get booklets about tours and all the buses are there."

"How will I know when I'm at the main station?"

"All the trains go there. You can't miss it."

My stepmother joined me at the counter. "I'll go with you."

"I thought you didn't want to."

"I'll go with you."

"All right."

The receptionist informed us, "The bus will leave in 5 minutes, but you can get there if you take the train."

"I doubt we can get there in five minutes." I turned to my stepmother. "Do you want to wait an hour?"

We were again encouraged. "You can get there in time if you go on the train."

We told Dad our plan to see the city. Not breathing well, he preferred to stay behind. Back on Rue de France, I stated my opinion, "I think we need to get on the train on this side."

"No, it's the other side."

What do I know about this city? Nothing! I followed across the tracks to the other platform.

Speaking French, my stepmother asked a man, "Where do we get the train to the main station?"

"The other side, but I'll help you get a ticket at this machine. It works the same."

Once in possession of two tickets, we hurried back to the other side. Already close to five minutes since we had left the hotel, we stepped onto the train. Carol noticed a man slide his ticket into a machine. She motioned. "Slide your ticket in here." She took hers back after the machine popped it back up then walked to a seated gentleman. In French, she asked, "Which is the main station?" The two spoke a few minutes before she returned to me. "He's getting off at the same station. We'll get off when he does."

Several stops down the line, we followed the man off the train. He spoke a few more words to Carol.

"Merci," I told him. *I'm so glad Carol is with me. I don't know what the receptionist was thinking.* This stop looked not one bit different than any of the others. As instructed, we walked in what we hoped was the correct direction. Assuming the bright orange building with giant gold plated flowerpots was the Office of Tourism, we circled it. No signage and, as you might have guessed, not open.

Way beyond our five-minute window, Carol asked for help from a passing young lady.

"Go across the street and get on the bus to the Office of Tourism. The tours are there."

Everybody has been so gracious. I'm very grateful, but we still don't know how to determine which is the correct bus. Carol and I stood at the bus stop. A bus pulled up. "Ask the driver," I suggested.

France

Two young ladies stood in the entry. Carol squeezed around them into the aisle. I stopped beside the driver. "Carol come up here, and ask him."

The man closed the door. Off we went to who knows where! Carol and I managed to maneuver around the young women, still standing in the way, and swapped places. In French, Carol spoke with the man operating the bus then turned to me. "We need bus 8. It's coming right behind this one."

We stopped at the next stop. I pointed to the front of the bus. "Is the number up there?"

"Yes."

I could have spoken with him in English! "How much do we owe you?" I asked.

"This one is gratis."

"Merci!"

We stepped off the bus expecting to immediately get on the next. "That one says 200. It isn't the one." Only a minute later, the bus numbered 8 pulled up.

Carol asked the driver, "Is this the bus that will take us to the tour buses?"

"Yes. I'll tell you when to get off."

I had figured it out. If you step onto a train or bus, it doesn't matter if you go one block or several kilometers, it's 1,50 €. I handed the driver a 5 € note. He returned 2 € in 20 cent coins: my punishment for not having correct change.

Several blocks down Promenade Des Anglais, the driver pointed, "They are right over there."

I could have walked, but I wouldn't have known where to go. The short ride was worth it. A tour bus already gathered up riders. Even though we were boarding the bus an hour later than planned to catch, I hoped we would have no further wait or struggle to find our destination. "Is this the bus to tour the city of Nice?"

"Yes, twenty Euros each."

"Will you be telling us about what we see in English?"

"You will hear in English when I give you your headset. Plug it in and tune to channel two."

I handed the driver a 50 note and then happily accepted a 10 € note and two sealed red plastic bags. Carol sat next to the window. I handed her one of the small bags. "Plug it in and turn to channel 2. I'm going to sit by that window." I slid into the seat beside the window across the bus then spent a few minutes unwrapping the twisted line of my hearing aid. Finally unwound, I plugged it in and turned to 2. *Silence. Probably not running yet because the bus is still parked.* I patiently waited. A few minutes and a few more passengers later, the tour was underway. I turned my phone to video and placed one of the earbuds beside the phone. *This will be great. When I get home, David can see and hear what it's all about.*

My error in seat selection soon became apparent. Sitting directly behind the driver, my forward view was completely obstructed. My second irritation was that the narrator didn't state where to look. Therefore, I was frequently unable to identify the object of interest. Still, I did see and videotape many attractions on my side of the bus.

The voice in my earbuds informed me that approximately 75% of the world's luxury yachts are anchored in the harbor of Nice at any given time. On the opposite side of the bus window, floated one of those yachts.

Provence

Royalty of many countries, who have wanted to enjoy the pleasant climate, have built palaces in Nice. The architecture of those buildings is varied based on the time of construction.

We passed Roman ruins, museums, and sculptures. One of which was a statue shaped like shoulders and a neck with a 15 X 15 X 15-meter block in place of its head! The sculpture is named *La Tête Au Carré* (The Square Head.) You would think the giant sculpture is just something to look at, but you would be wrong. It is the administrative office of *Bibliothèque* (Library). People outside can't see into the building. However, if you are standing outside the "Square Head", do not scratch your derriere. The staff members on one of the three floors in the neck or perhaps even all the way up on one of the four floors in the cube, do not share the inability to see through the walls. From inside the thirty-meter high building, one of them may be watching you.

After a two-hour tour, we returned to the place from which we had departed. "Carol, let's walk beside the sea."

"Are you sure? It's a long way."

I looked down the long curve of the Promenade Des Anglais to the far point across the Mediterranean Sea. "It can't be that far. I can see the airport."

I admired the art from road level and at the speed of foot travel.

France

We walked beyond the pink domed Russian Casino and other gambling establishments. A rack of postcards beckoned me. "I want more postcards." I perused the wide selection.

Carol asked one of the cashiers. "How far is the Ibis Hotel?"

"Forty minutes at an easy pace," the man assured her.

I picked out two cards then went inside the store crammed with tourist trinkets. *I want to get something for my sons and husband. None of this is anything any of them would love to have.*

I selected a coffee mug to use at work. The cashier retrieved a box in which to pack it. The store was empty.

I want my husband and sons to know that I'm thinking about them and that they're important to me. "One moment."

I went back to the shelf, selected three more mugs, turned around, and discovered that the line to the register now stretched across the store and out the door.

How did that happen? It's only been a few seconds?

I moved to the rear of the line. One person at a time, I moved toward the register. Another shift forward and I was only three people away. I stepped forward. I waited. When it was finally my turn the same young fellow, who had packaged my first mug called me over. He boxed my other three cups as I slid my card into the machine then waited while the system inquired of my bank back in America. 'Approved.'

I'm glad I notified my bank that I'd be using my card in France.

Provence

I rejoined Carol outside the store. "Let's cross over and walk beside the sea." We watched two men para-surfing. Their ride was not long; as soon as the wind failed to catch the parasail, both surfer and cloth sunk into the waves.

A set of stairs led down from the concrete walkway. "I want to touch the sea." I descended to the gray pebbles with white lines that littered the beach. I crunched across the stones to the water.

Only days before a wave had swept a man into the sea and then miraculously redeposited him still alive on the beach. *Once, well that did happen. Twice, I'm not taking the chance that I would survive such a ride.* In case any large swells rose from the sea floor, I cautiously monitored the Mediterranean.

If everybody who comes to this beach takes a pebble, will the beach be bare, or is there a never-ending supply? I decided not to attempt to answer my concern and grab for a smooth stone that had caught my eye. A wave covered it and then swept it away. I saw it again, but the wave coming in looked tall. I backed away in time to avoid the water that would only have wetted my shoes.

I'm not going to allow the sea to prevent me from acquiring an acceptable specimen. I again attempted to best the waves to retrieve a pebble with an exceptional pattern of white lines. Water splashed my toes, but I captured my prize. The stone that had lived in the sea slid into my pocket and, happily, my fingers had touched the Mediterranean.

France

An hour of walking beside the sea and the airport didn't appear to have drawn much nearer. "Maybe we should try to catch a bus."

"You said you wanted to walk."

"All right, we'll keep going. Let me tighten my shoelaces." I put my foot on the rail beside a piece of plastic trash. I looked down to pull my laces. *Those are fresh roses, and that package is tied to the rail. I think some man, planning to take his love on a walk beside the sea, has tied them here. 'Oh, what is this my love?' he will ask when he gets to his carefully placed flowers. Down on bended knee to pick up the flowers for his lady he will look up into her eyes, declare his love, and asked her to spend her life with him. Maybe not, but why else would they be there.* I chose to believe in the love I had imagined and clung to the idea that romance remains. *I hope nobody else finds those flowers, decides to take a bunch of free roses, and dashes a man's plans.*

My toes hurt, and my hair was wet with the mist of rain and the spray of the sea, but how many times might a person have the chance to walk where I was walking?

As I continued, a blister grew under my toe, and the rain came in earnest. I opened my umbrella. The wind immediately turned it inside out. *I choose to get wet in favor of saving the integrity of the umbrella that isn't going to serve its function anyway.* I drew it closed. A minute in the rain, Carol dashed under the glass bus stop. I joined her. "Let's take the bus. It's been over an hour since the store. I don't know what that man's idea of a slow walk is, but I think we've been going pretty fast, the airport still looks far away, and now it's raining."

When the walk signal notified us that it was safe, we crossed and stepped onto the next bus. I deposited 3 Euros in the shallow indentation beside the driver. The driver handed Carol two tickets, which she fed into the machine as I gratefully sat in the seat. Ten minutes and probably five miles later, we arrived at our hotel. I calculated in my head. We must have been ten miles away when I had decided to walk to our hotel by the airport. It had appeared to be just up the road at the far end of a long curve.

In our room, I suggested, "I'd like Mediterranean Pizza tonight."

"Why and what's on a Mediterranean Pizza?" my father asked.

"Pizza is from Italy, and we're right here beside it. I don't know what is on them, but we walked past some restaurants and the pizzas smelt good."

Carol suggested, "I saw several places on Rue de France. We can go look and decide if we want to go later."

We took the street beside the hotel. Dirt and bits of jade plant still littered the pavement. The car, however, was gone. "There's a sign that says Pizza." I pointed a short way down Rue de France.

"It doesn't look nice."

I followed Carol up the road upon which we had left the hotel. A few blocks later, only apartment buildings surrounded us. We crossed the street and headed back. Ahead, a throng of men stood and sat on the sidewalk outside a bar. *Maybe we should cross back to the other side.* Carol fearlessly threaded between the men. *I'm not letting her pass that way alone.* Unmolested we returned to Rue de France.

I filmed a flight of swallows playing, circling, clustering, and then spreading apart but never knocking each other out of the sky.

Provence

Just beyond the swallows, a restaurant's exterior wall of metal slats stood open. We went inside and looked at the menu on the wall. Chicken on most of them. Cheese and fresh cream on every one of them. "Would you like to come back to this one?" I asked.

"Let's keep looking."

At the end of the block of restaurants, we looked both ways down the long straight road with the train tracks in the middle. No cars or trains. On the other side, we resumed our hunt for the perfect pizzeria. The next possibility had the menu posted outside. We looked it over. "What about this one?"

"No."

"Why not?"

"They don't serve wine."

After looking over every restaurant within easy walking distance, I concluded that we were in the fast food section of Nice. I was pretty sure that wine was not going to be an offering in any of them. At the last pizzeria before arriving back where we started, I looked at the menu hanging on the wall outside. The picture of the "Chef's choice" looked good; crumbles of sausage, lovely looking olives, and lots of cheese. "I'm going to order one and take it back to the room." I went inside. "Do you speak English?"

"A little."

"33 cm Chef's Choice," I pointed to the exit, "to go."

"OK." The man set to work. My mouth watered as I anticipated the scrumptious pizza to come.

Carol and I sat at an empty table and watched the soccer game on the large TV screen on the wall. Speaking in French, Carol chatted with a man also watching the game. Ten minutes passed. I watched my pizza go into a box. I paid the man and hurried through the wind, hoping all the warmth would not be sucked from my culinary treasure.

In our room, I opened the box. *Wonderful, it's still warm. What's that in the middle? An egg! Cracked open, poured on, and cooked with the pizza. This pizza looks nothing like the picture outside the restaurant. I won't criticize without trying it.*

My taste buds anticipated the succulent treat. I avoided the egg and took a bite of crunchy crust, topped with sausage links cut into pieces, and black olives... *Oh my gosh!*

My teeth were prevented from making contact with each other by a hard object. *This is horrible!*

I spit the conglomeration into a napkin. *The olives have pits!*

I sampled a sausage only portion. *Not much better.*

I tore off and ate a piece with egg. *Nasty!*

I pitted the olives and placed them back in the cheese beside the chunks of meat. Being wasteful is not something I'm comfortable with, so I left the portion with the egg in the box and managed to get down three of the small slices. Unable to go on, no matter how much I hate wasting, I closed the box. *Very disappointing. Still, I've had so many wonderful meals. I'm not going to be upset.*

I stayed in the room and worked on my project while Dad and Carol went down to the hotel restaurant. When they returned, I asked, "How was it? What did you get?"

"They had even fewer choices than yesterday. We had bread and cheese."

I'd already had plenty of those two items, and I hadn't missed a savory meal. "Sorry guys." Already showered and in my PJs, I got under the covers and left the waking world behind.

France

Return

The wakeup call sounded. I didn't hurry to cross the room to answer. Four steps and I had silenced the annoyance. Carol flipped on the light. Once dressed, we quickly packed the few items not already stowed. "Where is your door key?" Carol asked.

"It's there on the table."

"This one is your father's."

He was indisposed at the moment. "Hum. I'll look." I dragged out every item in my hip bag. It wasn't there. I squeezed the items back inside then emptied my carryon on the bed. It wasn't there. I looked at my suitcase. *Surely, I didn't pack it in there.* "Are you sure one of those isn't mine?"

Carol called out, "Oliver, do you have your key?"

"I do. It's in my pocket."

I told myself, *I should have asked before I dumped everything.* "Thanks, Dad," was all I said.

With plenty of time, we stood before the same receptionist. "We should only have meals to pay for."

"Fifty-nine Euros," the woman informed us in the language I understood.

That's what she told us was the cost of breakfast for three. "Did she get everything? What about your cheese and bread?"

The young woman looked at her screen. "That's included."

How could that be? One or the other quoted price is wrong. It isn't my business. I said no more.

"Please call a taxi for us," Carol requested.

We stood in the cool, morning breeze and waited. *I hope the taxi gets here quickly. I don't know how long Dad can stand or me for that matter.* I stood on the side road and looked for the previously smashed car.

"I think the taxi will stop at the front of the hotel." Dad walked around the corner.

Surely he'll get off the road and give us a safe place to load up. I remained where I stood, the street on which the damaged car was no longer located.

"He's here!" Dad called out. Expertly, quickly, and safely loaded and on our way, I decided *I shouldn't believe I've got any valid idea about what's going to happen.*

In the airport, we walked to a woman beside a self-service station. I handed over my passport. The woman scanned it then handed it back. "Please take a seat until 8 am. You can go through at that time."

"Do you see the request for a wheelchair?" Dad asked.

"Yes. Please have a seat. It will be brought when it's closer to your time."

We did as instructed. However, we did not wait patiently. Other people went to the same lady or worked the self-service consoles themselves. They walked through the gate with boarding passes. I went back to the gatekeeper. "Can we go through now?"

"When does your flight leave?"

"10:10"

"Come back at 10:08"

I informed Carol and Dad of the stated allowed time for passage through the guarded gate. "Surely that's wrong. He must mean 8:10."

At 8:00, my father shuffled over and asked for a wheelchair.

"At 10:08 you can go through and ask for it at the counter."

"You're wrong. You said eight minutes after 10, and that would only give us two minutes before the plane is in the air. Do you mean 8:10; as in ten minutes after eight?"

Provence

"Oh yes. I'm sorry. I said that wrong."

Dad hobbled back without a cane or a wheelchair. "It's not many more minutes."

A woman approached with a wheelchair. "Over here!" I called out.

"State your name."

My father did so and got the reply, "I'm sorry. This one is not for you." The woman walked away. *How did somebody else manage to get one.*

At 8:10, we again tried to pass into the forbidden land on the other side of the gate. "Come through."

People already stood in line. *How is anybody already here? I wonder if Dad or I will be able to stand as long as might be required.* Happily, the line moved quickly. Dad stepped up to the counter. "Please request my wheelchair."

By the time our bags were on the conveyor belt, the wheelchair and attendant had arrived. Again, Carol and I followed the fast-moving person pushing Dad before us. I placed my carryon bags in the plastic bin and slid them onto the conveyor belt. On the other side of the metal detector, I was asked, "Are these your bags?" I acknowledged ownership. "Please step over here."

I stood on the other side of the belt from the guard removing objects from my bag. A second guard blocked me from behind. A third stood at my left. Several men and women attended to the others in the line to my right. "You can't have this," said the man with my 7 € bottle of wine in his hand.

"What can I do?"

"Put it in your checked bag."

"My checked bag is long gone."

"You can abandon it."

"There isn't any other way?"

The man walked away with my wine. He returned with a bottle-sized cardboard box and some papers. He filled out the paper then was no longer able to speak English or explain what he was doing. He attempted to close the box. It did not fasten securely. *I'm sure that's going to pop open.* He pointed to a line on the paper. "Sign here."

Wow! I might be consenting to execution here! "What is this?"

"You pick up later."

I signed my name. "Should I fill in my address?"

The man pulled a tag off the box. He handed me a pamphlet and the tag that matched its counterpart still attached to the cardboard transportation container. "What do I do?" The man walked away with my very poorly packaged wine.

My father's handler appeared agitated. I was costing him potential tips while they waited for me. *Oh well. There's no way to figure anything out right now.* I folded the tag inside the pamphlet and shoved it into my pocket. I walked away and then dutifully followed the wheelchair to the elevator where we piled in. Deposited by the gate and then left to our own defenses, I purchased pastries, coffee, and orange juice for the three of us. We sat at a tiny table and consumed our breakfast before I went searching for earrings to fill the void left by my failure to acquire the earrings in Tourtour. I found no earrings or anything else worthy of purchase.

I returned just in time. The same woman who had left us beside the gate was headed to the front of the line with Dad in the wheelchair. I shielded my view of the disgusted glances of the people we were bypassing. I handed over my passport and boarding pass.

France

Before long, the plane carried us through the air toward Paris. Once we had disembarked, we were whisked to a bus then across Charles De Gaulle Airport to our departure gate. I again searched for earrings but found none. I settled for two boxes of chocolates to share with my family and co-workers back home.

All three of us, in the middle seats of the premium economy section, examined our surrounding. More leg room, a bigger screen in the back of the seat in front of us, a plastic-wrapped blanket, and an unwrapped pillow in the seat. Streams of people struggled along the narrow aisle to the economy seats behind us. My father remarked, "There must be a lot of seats back there."

I, however, immediately set to searching the movie selections. I hoped to find a particular one. There it is! I queued it up then continued to peruse the selections. After selecting every movie that looked interesting, I pressed play on my primary choice.

"Are you watching a movie already?" Carol asked.

"Yes, I want to finish the one I watched on the way to France." I took the wrapped wet wipe offered by the flight attendant and removed what was most likely billions of germs picked up during my travels through the airport.

Not long after departure, we were given meals of cold monkfish, hot chicken in mustard sauce, a vegetable medley, and spinach mixed into pureed potatoes. With it came a pear turnover of sorts, a small wedge of camembert cheese, a roll, and a pat of butter. I was also offered a choice of water, coffee, tea, red or white wine, soda of various flavors, or fruit juice. As we ate, I examined our flight path on the screen and talked with my parents.

Two movies later, we were brought a foil covered serving of orange juice in a plastic container.

Thinking we would be first off and quickly escorted through Dulles Airport, I donned my coat and stepped into the aisle.

"Please step over here." An attendant pulled us from the mass of people about to swarm off the plane.

What! I don't have wine this time!

"Your wheelchair is not here yet."

So, the man who needs a wheelchair is left standing stooped over in the small space in front of the first row in our section. A comfortable seat in the vacated first class area two steps ahead not even offered as the rear of the plane emptied. "Your chair is here now."

Even though she could have offered my father a seat, it wasn't the flight attendant who had been holding the wheelchairs hostage. I did not comment. In the exit ramp, a row of empty wheelchairs sat lined up by the wall. I asked which of them was looking for my father. I stated his name. This time, any of them was permitted to help any of the people there, so the young man beside whom we stood helped my father into his chair.

Provence

Once again rolled past the lines, we were brought directly to a side station. "Do you have anything to declare?" asked the customs man.

"One bottle of wine."

"Only one?"

Maybe none. "Yes, only one."

The man in the glass cage stuck a yellow label to the back of each of our passports and passed them back. Off we went to baggage pickup. "Where would I pick up my bottle of wine?" I asked the man pushing my father.

"Try over there." He pointed to a counter across the room. "I'll get the bags of your parents." I remained beside the carousel. Bags popped from the chute onto the circular track. On and on they came until they did not. Still, minus our bags, I looked at our helper. "More will come," he informed me.

Another batch arrived, still without bringing ours. We waited again. "There's mine!" I grabbed the bag with the bright green and pink ribbons. I started away with my luggage in tow.

"Leave it here. I'll get it on a cart," offered the young man still waiting for our other bags.

I hurried to the counter where I hoped I could claim my box, hopefully not containing a broken bottle. I handed the woman my claim tag. "Do I pick this up here?"

"What's this?" With a bewildered look, she examined the small plastic tag.

"My claim ticket."

"I don't know anything about this. What is it for?"

"A bottle of wine in a small cardboard box."

"Oh, irregular size. Go over there." She pointed to the opposite side of the large room.

I passed my family already with all our bags on a cart. "She said to go over there."

At a short conveyor belt with a stroller beside it, I held out my ticket. "Do I claim this here?"

"What's that?"

Does nobody here know their own procedures? "My claim ticket."

"For what?"

"It's a small box with a bottle of wine."

"That wouldn't be here. Try over there." The man directed me towards the same counter from which I had previously been ejected.

"They just told me to come here." Another young man came over. I explained again.

He looked at the tag and the pamphlet. "We don't have any service like this. You should go to the website listed here."

The baggage claim area wasn't the place to pull out my laptop, and everybody was clearly ready to leave. "Never mind."

Carol told me, "Add some money to our tip. You've kept this man from helping others."

"Of course." I had previously decided I would do so. I dug through my wallet as I followed.

Outside, in cold drizzle, we were taken to a valet assigning people to a super shuttle. I pressed some bills into my father's hand. "For the man."

Dad held out the money. "Thank you so much and sorry for taking up so much time."

"That's quite all right." Without counting, our escort pushed the money into his pocket and hurried away.

With Dad still in the wheelchair, but now under the supervision of the shuttle loader, we waited for our assignment.

"This one please."

No ramp! "Is there a ramp?" I asked.

France

"I can get in all right." Dad stood up, took the few steps across the sidewalk, and then pulled himself up into the van. He slid across the seat.

"Do you want me to take your other bags?" the driver asked.

The night before, I had compressed the file containing this story and had attempted to email it to myself. Even compressed, the file had been too large. Therefore, I had no copy of the information in any other location. I didn't want to take a chance of my laptop being damaged. "No, but thank you." In the space between my legs and the seat in front, I wedged my bag on top of my feet. With a businessman from France and another from South Africa, we traveled from Dulles to Alexandria where we were deposited at our front door.

I fired up my laptop and navigated to the website listed on the pamphlet given to me in Nice, France. I entered my code and read my choices.

With my claim tag and identification, pick up my package at the airport in Nice. *That's not a feasible choice.*

With my claim tag and a power of attorney from myself, my agent can pick up my package in Nice. *Also, no!*

Abandon my package either by not claiming within 21 days or selecting to abandon at this time. *With this choice, I'm giving my permission for the company to do with my package as they choose. I'd rather not.*

Pay to have my package shipped. *The box wasn't even closed properly. I'd probably get it smashed or no longer even in the box, and I bet that would be expensive. Drat! I guess I've given somebody a bottle of rosé wine.*

After having a wonderful adventure in France, even without my wine, I slept, happy to have taken a marvelous trip and also to be home in America.